The Adventures of Coolaidnate

Chapter 1

I remember when I first thought about the idea of becoming a truck driver; it was in 1982, the same year my maternal grandmother passed away. We went down to her funeral that year. You see, my grandmother raised me in a small town in Florida called Hilliard until I was eighteen. After that, I moved up to Rochester, New York, and I have lived there from then until now. I have been wondering since I was in Job Corps, back in 1969, how to get into truck driving. One day, a friend of the young lady I was dating at the time told me about a school where I could get free training and how to get a grant to get into the school. I was accepted in 1982. That was the year my grandmother passed away. We went down to Hilliard for her funeral. After the funeral, we went back to Rochester, and later that next month, I started the class. The school was in a town outside of Syracuse, New York, called Lafayette. The next first few days were spent in class working on hours-of-service logbooks, which covered what hours of service were and had four sections: Off Duty, Sleeper Berth, Driving, and On-duty times. Then, we had hazardous materials and placard signs (you would need these signs to warn of the possible dangers of the load you had onboard). We also learned defensive driving, which covered the five smith system keys: **1.** Aim High Steering, **2.** Get the Big picture, **3.** Keep your eyes moving, **4.** Leave yourself an out, and **5.** Make sure they see you. Along with the paperwork, shifting patterns and even a simulator was included. After that, we started going outside to get familiar with the trucks; and I must say, that was something special for me. You see, up until then, I had never gotten in a big truck and sat in the driver's seat! When I was a kid, I used to watch trucks pass through my hometown in Hilliard and listen to the sound of their engines as the driver's changed gears, leaving town until I could not hear them anymore, thinking to myself how much I would love to be one of them. I would even pretend to be a truck driver with the top of a trash can and a stick, shifting gears and steering like I was going somewhere. And now here I am, training to be a truck driver, really driving trucks for a living. The teacher was telling us about all the gauges and controls on the dashboard. These trucks had so many gauges that I didn't know if I would be able to remember them all if we were to have a test after this! And then he said, "CRANK IT UP!" I was like, *what?* And he repeated, as he looked up at me, "CRANK IT UP!" I was apprehensive about that, and I was thinking, *what if something goes wrong? What if the truck started to move? What if it backed up into something?* He was way down there on the ground, and I was up there; his face was only as high as the steps of the truck! He assured me that it would be safe, so I started it; it sounded so powerful, yet it was under control. I was shown all the gauges and what they were supposed to read and where all the controls were located. And all fifteen of us, one at a time, got in and did the same thing, then went back to the classroom. At the end of the day, we all went back to the hotel, got something to eat at a nearby restaurant, and later went to bed. This went on for about a week until the day came when we would start operating these large trucks. We went out to the back of the school, where the trucks were, in a big field with all kinds of obstacles, to practice maneuvering the trucks in and out of and around each obstacle to get a feel for how the trucks handled and what to do to get them to go where we wanted them to go. That went on for a week or so, and then the day came when we were going on the road! There were four of us in each truck with a trainer, taking turns using what we were taught in class and on the obstacle field. When I returned from a training run the next day, another truck from my class arrived, and we found out that a young lady was driving, and she panicked and ripped the stick shift right out of the transmission… wow. The day finally came for our school test; we had to drive through the city, making turns and backing into docks as if we were about to be loaded. We also practiced interstate driving and parallel parking on the driver's side (which is called the see side) and on the right side (which is called the blind side). At about the end of my test, I was told to make a very tight right turn to get on the highway. As I was completing the turn, my right trailer tire ran over the curb… an automatic failure! I felt so defeated, but I was told to take that as my warning, and the state test would be easier; just watch my curbs! On the day of the state test, everything went well. I passed, I had completed my Tractor Trailer Training… and I was finally a Tractor Trailer Driver!

Chapter 2

When I got back home to Rochester, I had such a challenging time finding a job. You see that year, there was a trucker strike going on, and it seemed as though all the other truck drivers with more experience than myself were beating me to all the available jobs. After about two years, I finally found one that would have hired me... but they said because of my lack of truck driving history, I would have to go back to truck driving school. The last time I went, I received a grant from CETA (Comprehensive Employment and Training Act) but this time, I had to get a loan. I went through the same process that I did two years ago. The loan did not cover all my needs, though, so I had to produce ways to eat. I had a roommate, and he produced some ideas for making some extra funds to carry us through the lean times. We started selling squares of paper, saying that they were blotter acid. We sold them to the college students. What got me was that they kept coming back and saying that it was the best that they ever had. After finishing school, I found out that the company that was going to put me to work was no longer available. So, I was on the hunt again! But after a while, I finally found one! It was with Ryder Truck Rental as what was called a "Hiker!" We picked up and delivered trucks to customers and from shop to shop; that was fun, and I was doing something I liked. I remember on one trip, there were about three or four of us headed out to pick up some trucks out of town. We were all in a van, and the van had a bad fume leak. I got sleepy and decided to go to the back of the van and lie down; we had a way to go, so why not? As I was lying there relaxing and thinking about the ride, suddenly, I felt so at peace. There was no sound, and I was looking at the stars, not from a distance but within them, moving through them by myself, so calm, so peaceful, and I remembered thinking, *this is so peaceful, I can only think of one thing that could be this peaceful and that is...* then I stopped, but my mind kept on with the thought... *Death!* I remembered asking, *am I dead?* And I heard a soft voice beside me say, "You don't have to be." That made me so happy that it woke me up. I felt a tingle in my body, as if my blood was just starting to flow again, and I was so happy because I thought I was dead, or at least dying. The guys in the front of the van knew nothing; they were still carrying on like nothing had happened. One day, not long after that, Ryder let me know that a company named Duffy Motts needed some trucks, and another company that placed workers, like a temporary agency, wanted to hire some of us. After being hired, I found out that I was on the night shift, so the first night, I had to get a ride from another driver. When we got there, we found that the day crew was just getting off, and we were to take over, so the guy who had the truck before me told me what truck I had and what I needed to do. The truck was a brand-new Kenworth cab-over with a sleeper from 1984, and it was in 1984 that I began driving the truck! It had only about eighty-nine miles on the dash and still had that new truck smell. We were at a warehouse in a town in New York named Hamlin; we had to go empty to a town about forty-five miles away called Williamson to get loaded with apple products to bring back to Hamlin to the warehouse, and then unload and repeat. We pulled out in a line of four trucks, and I was the last one; I had to keep up because I didn't know the way on my own. I had a ten-speed transmission with a short stick shift, and it shifted so smoothly that I felt like I was a pro. We started out on Route 19 south, and I was seeing the world from a different point of view, from high above the cars and people. As I drove down the road, I came upon a curve that banked to the right; I downshifted to a lower gear and started into the curve, then I sped up slightly because I remembered from school that you should never let the trailer push you around a curve. It felt like I was flying a jet plane into a right bank; shoot, I even enjoyed it. As I came out of the curve, I started shifting again; I took the curve at 35 miles an hour in sixth gear. I built my speed up to forty-five miles an hour and rolled up to a red light that turned green just before I got there, so I put on my left turn signal and made a left turn onto 104 eastbound. On my way, I kept going over some of the things my teachers in school told me to do as I was driving aim high steering (looking far enough up the road to spot hazards), look in my side-view mirrors to make sure my wheels are tracking in my lane, and watch for over-hangs. As I approached Lake Avenue, I could see Kodak Park on my left; I remembered when I was employed there back in 1974. After I passed Kodak, I went across the Genesee River bridge, continuing I crossed I-590, staying on 104-East, then I crossed the Bay Bridge. A little after that, we arrived in Williamson, where Duffy Motts was located. We parked the trucks and went upstairs to get our assignments; we found the person in charge, a lady, and there were four other ladies in the office. We were introduced to everyone and then given our instructions. We stood by as the guys on the loading dock began to load our trailers, and then we were on our way back to Hamlin to be unloaded. This time, I was not the last truck in line but about truck number three. I was watching the truck in front of me as he changed lanes, made turns, stops, and starts. He seemed to move along smoothly; I felt that the driver behind me was watching my driving too; I could be wrong, but that is what I was feeling! We had a lot of red lights to go through, and finely we arrived back in Hamlin and talked to the Forman to find out where he wanted us to dock. I watched the guys on the forklifts while they unloaded the trailers two pallets at a time until it was empty and then back to get another load. One day there was a slight change; we had to make a stop on the way back to get reloaded. We stopped at a glass factory in a town called Brockport and got a load of glass to take back to Williamson, and then at Williamson, we unloaded the glass and reloaded it for a return trip to Hamlin. On Friday came payday. After looking at my check, I realized that becoming a tractor-trailer driver was one of the best ideas I had ever made! This went on until the apple season was over. During the off season, I went on unemployment and looked for another job. After the second off season, I found a job over the road.

Chapter 3

It was a company in Daleville, IN, and the ad was in the paper; they needed a team to drive over the road. Two of us signed up, and they tested us in Rochester; up until then, I was driving 45-foot trailers, but they had 48-foot ones! But we passed the test; my partner was from the same company I was with before this: Ryder Truck Rental. So, we went to Daleville, Indiana, for orientation, where we were prepared for over-the-road driving by their rules, meeting the dispatchers, and getting our assignments. Then, we received a truck: a 1984, white Peterbilt cab-over tractor and a 48-foot trailer; we were now Tractor Trailer Drivers! After being dispatched, we picked up the load and was on our way to El Paso, Texas. We left the terminal and got on I-69 and headed south. My teammate, Tom, started driving first; I was so happy knowing that my career had finally started. I remember being amazed as we came to Indianapolis because I had never been there before. I heard so much about it, but there I was... looking at its buildings and some of the people and cars going on their way, doing what they do, going to work, going downtown, possibly to movies, stores or wherever, just milling around. We entered the bypass I-465 south and onto I-65 South towards Louisville, where were there was a 76-truck stop where we stopped for something to eat and a bathroom break. So, we got off at exit 348 in Angola, Indiana, and found a parking spot; there were a lot of places to park. Tom lined up for a spot and backed in. This was my first time at a real truck stop other than that little one in my hometown in Florida; this place was bigger and had a lot of parking spots, a place to eat, a store, and not to mention, a line of fuel islands for trucks and cars. We went in and found the restrooms; there were multiple stalls and places to wash your hands, and I noticed that there were even places to take showers; *how cool.* We met other truck drivers and talked to them and found out that there were drivers from a little bit of everywhere! But then we had to get back on the road; walking past the store, I saw some of the products that were on sale, and I was thinking to myself, *how convenient.* When I get some money, I see a few things that I would not mind buying. Going through the parking lot, I paid attention to some of the trucks in the lot, and I thought to myself, *this is what I want to do, drive big trucks and go all over the United States and just be free.* When we made it back to the truck and got back on I-65 South, I went into the sleeper berth and got some sleep. When I woke up, we were coming into Memphis, Tennessee; another state and city I had never been to before. We found another 76 truck-stop and stopped for a bite to eat. And then, on the road again. As we crossed the Mississippi River, I saw more truck stops on the west Memphis side, and I thought to myself, *what could they be doing down there?* There were a lot of trucks down there, and truck stops on both sides of the bridge, but we kept on going until we reached Arkansas on I-40 West; from there, we got on I-30 West to Little Rock. It was now my turn to take the wheel. I drove for a while then we came to a rest area. The off-ramp for the rest area was on the left side; that was new to me; all the other ones I had seen so far was on the right side of the road. After a quick bathroom break, I was ready to go. As I was getting some gear, Tommy, my partner, decided to crawl back in the sleeper berth for some sleep. A couple of hours or so later, I arrived at Hope, Arkansas, where there was a scale to weigh trucks. I fallowed the other trucks onto the scale, and then on my way. Each sign I saw of nearby towns, I wondered, *what goes on there? What are the people like? and these cars... Where are they going?* And I also saw other tractor-trailers and wondered where they were going. I noticed a car in front of me with New York plates, way out here in Arkansas. I wondered how far they were going, if they were visiting someone or going to the store. It was a man and a woman who were laughing and talking about something. There was also a dog in the back looking out of the window with his tongue hanging out. I kept on rolling and soon crossed the Texas state line; Rockwell, Texas, driving on a roadway that looked like a bridge, heading for Dallas. As I got closer to Dallas, I could see the skyline, and I felt excited; it was night, and the lights fascinated me; they were so beautiful; different shapes and colors. There was even one that looked like a giant disco ball. We got on I-635 and headed south until we reached I-20, then we headed west going through Fort Worth; we kept going west. After a while, I started seeing places that reminded me of some old west movies where the cowboys and Indigenous people would battle over the land and water holes. The rest areas had makeshift teepees to get out of the sun. When we got to the Pecos, it was time for Tom to take over, so we took a quick break and then switched places. I sat in the passenger seat for a while; after that, I crawled in the sleeper berth. When I awoke, we were coming into El Paso, close to the Mexican border. This was like a vacation to me; I had never been so close to Mexico before, so everything I saw fascinated me. We got there a little early, so we went to a 76 truck stop on Horizon Blvd. I wanted to see so much more, but it was not enough time. I was working, so it was time to unload and reload before continuing to the next location. After a quick meal and a bathroom break, we were on our way to finish the run. We docked the truck to get unloaded and went into the dock area to watch. Soon we were done, so we called dispatch for our next run. We waited for about an hour or so, then we were told that the next load was down in Laredo, Texas; about 604 miles away, empty! So, we took out the map and chartered a course for Laredo, and we were on our way! On the way to Laredo, we passed the Uniroyal Tire testing grounds, and they had a test going on right then. I saw about three cars driving on a dirt trail following one another, dust everywhere. They were going in and out around cactus plants and close to a fence separating the highway from the desert; I watched until they were out of view. I will always remember that sight and will maybe start buying that brand of tire. I saw a bunch of ranches looking like the old west, with horses and cows. I even saw some tumbleweeds blowing across the road. I felt like I stepped back in time; I had seen a lot in Texas those last few days! Another thing I saw on the way to Laredo was a Bull Hauler, which is a tractor-trailer carrying cows. It was so far back; all I could see was its lights in my mirror. And then I started hearing wheels. When I looked back, the truck had gotten close enough for me to make out it was a tractor-trailer, and by that time, it was starting to past me. It was moving so fast, I was barely able to see what it was carrying, and just as fast as it got to me, it was passing me and pulling away at a high rate of speed. It passed me as though I was parked, and before I knew it, all I could see was taillights, and then it was gone! Tom told me that it was a Bull hauler, and they drive like that all the time. It was starting to get lighter as we started to arrive to Laredo. The destination was located on Scott Street, and we were told that the load would not be ready until the afternoon. So, we decided to go across the border into Mexico. The border was on the other side of a bridge that crossed the Rio Grande River. I heard a lot about that river in movies and television shows, and now there I was… South of the Rio Grande! The first thing I saw was small shops on both sides of the street, selling all kinds of goods from food and clothing to arts and crafts. I had on an old pair of dress boots with the souls coming apart, and a young man asked me if I would like to have them polished, and I told him that the boots were coming apart, but he insisted that he would be able to make them look so good that all I would have to do is get the souls replaced and they'd be as good as new. So, I let him, and boy was he right; they shined like brand new! I also bought a bottle of Tequila and a Sombrero for a souvenir, and I found an American Burger place and stopped in for a bite because I did not see anything else that I wanted to eat. But it was getting close to the time to get our load and head back north. Crossing back across the river, we had to stop at the border guard station. The guard then asked us where we were born, and then we were on our way to the truck! On my way, I noticed that the highway (I-35) ended right at the bridge, mile marker zero… The end of the United States. The beginning of The Country of Mexico! I remember thinking to myself, *one day, I am going to have to come back. I know that there is much more that I would like to see here.* Back at the loading dock, we found out the load was going to New Orleans, Louisiana! *Oh, I like this, I am seeing a lot out here, a lot!* On the way, we came across another border check point where they looked under the truck and brought the dogs out to go over the truck, looking for people trying to leave the country by stowing away in the back of trucks and for drugs being smuggled into the United States. After clearing the border check point, we headed north on I-35 until we reached I-10 and headed east.

Chapter 4

New Orleans.

After we got on I-10 East in San Antonio, Texas, we found a TA-Truck Stop where we got something to eat. After that, I climbed back into the sleeper birth for some sleep while Tom took the wheel. It appeared as soon as I got to sleep, my teammate's driving disturbed me by finding every bump in the road. I laid there for a while and tried to put up with it until I just could not take anymore. I stuck my head out of the sleeper-birth and asked Tom if he could just try to miss at least one or two of the bumps in the highway. He said that the highway was just raggedy, and he could not. So, I told him to stop at the first store he could, and when he did, I got a quart of beer and chugged it down right away. When I woke up, we were in New Orleans on Airport Road, where we were to unload. In New Orleans, I noticed that there were a lot of Black businesses, Limousines, Taxi cabs, and shuttle busses… I thought to myself, *I would love to live down here!* We got unloaded and then checked into a hotel for the weekend. I felt weird being in a hotel room with a guy, but at least it had two beds! We then heard music coming from downstairs… good music too. We figured since we were there, why not look to see what it was about. When we arrived at the club, we found that it was jumping, that they were getting down to some nice jazz, zydeco, and blues, so we bought some beers and sat down to enjoy the music. I spotted some young women, and we went over to talk with them; it went well, and we spent some time together! That night before we parted, one of the young ladies gave me her phone number. Back in the Hotel, Tom and I talked about the events of the evening and went to sleep. We got up about eleven or so and talked some more about the past night, then I produced the idea of contacting the young women again, so we called and was invited to come over where they lived! We used the tractor as transportation for the trip, like our personal car. When we arrived, I realized that the lights from the previous night, as well as the way they were dressed, had played a trick on my eyes, and they were not as attractive as I had thought. I mean, they weren't exactly ugly, but they seemed more attractive that night. I lost interest in pursuing a physical relationship with them and turned the visit into a get high venture; I asked if they knew of anywhere to get some smoke, and they both answered yes and took us to get some, and even smoked with me because Tom did not want to get high. The girls and I got our high on and talked until Tom, was ready to go. We said our goodbyes and went on our way back to the hotel, where we got into our beds and watched TV for a while, and then went to sleep. The next morning, we went to pick up our cargo and left New Orleans and headed back north. On the way, I was driving when I noticed what looked like cages shaped like little domes in the ponds along the road. I found out later that they were crayfish traps, and that is how they catch crayfish. On the way north, we went through Mississippi, and I saw cotton in the fields for the first time in my life. I thought about getting some for a souvenir, but I decided against it and kept moving. When we got to Meridian, Mississippi, we stopped at a pilot truck stop, and I teased Tom about the name of the street; Tommy Web Drive because his first name is Tommy. We went to the cat scale to make sure that our weight was right, good thing we did… because we were about 2000 pounds over on the back of the trailer; we had to move it to the front! After a while, we figured out how to move the weight to the right place by moving the tandems. First, we moved them back some, but we moved them too far. Then, we moved them back up some, and now they were right back to where they were before the first time. So, we moved them back some more, and that was too much, and we were starting to get a little frustrated plus, it was costing us money; the first one was $5.00, then $1.00 for the next ones. The last time, we got it right on the money! After that, we were ready for a shower and something to eat, so we got our free shower tickets because of the times we fueled up at the other pilot truck stops on our run, and after that, we went to Subway where I got a tuna sub, a bag of salt and vinegar chips, and a macadamia cookie with a large root beer drink. We ate and then went back to the truck to continue our way.

Chapter 5

For our next rest point, we stopped in Tuscaloosa, Alabama. At another pilot truck stop, after a quick restroom break, I went back into the sleeper birth while Tom took the wheel. When I woke up, we were going through Atlanta, Georgia. I remember seeing five-lane highways in Atlanta's beltway, and I am told that trucks are not supposed to be in the three left lanes of them! I saw a building that looked like a police station, and there was a helicopter on top of it. The traffic was ridiculous, bumper-to-bumper traffic all around me; I felt like I was in that movie Star Wars; vehicles were going around me on both sides. When one pulled out from in front of me, another one moved right in! Like water displacement, and it was like that for an extended period. I saw the Coca-Cola company on my left, and after a while, we were leaving Atlanta on I-75 North, now headed towards Marietta, Georgia. Tom and I started talking about CB handles. I decided to go with Black Cowboy, and Tom went with Captain Tee. I bought a cowboy hat like the one worn by Jerry Reed in Smoky and the Bandit, with little pendants. I had one for Peter Built and about two more. I also had a big belt buckle with a truck on it, and those boots that I had shined up in Mexico, with blue jeans; they looked like cowboy boots! And Captain Tee mentioned that he could get a citizen band radio (CB) when we get back home. So, Captain Tee said that he was going to get some sleep and leave it to me. As I was driving, I was thinking of how this is an illustrious career for me. I love driving, and it gives me time to just think! While captain Tee was sleeping, I can go over things in my mind like my plans and remember the events of the past. I had been through a lot of places so far, some that I would not mind living in, especially New Orleans! It is a lot like Florida; warm, next to the water and seafood… my kind of town! I was passing another truck; a J.B. Hunt truck; there was a lady driving it, not bad looking either. I thought to myself, *what if she were my future wife?* We could drive as a team and have all the money going into one house, buy a truck, and live in it, going all over America and staying in hotels from time to time as we loved and make love. But then again, maybe not. I often had thoughts like that. *Anyway, I must get my head back in the game now and head on up the road!* It was time to stop and get some fuel and something to eat. As we were getting ready to leave the truck stop, there was a truck that was unhooked from a trailer and setting a little in front of it. I could not help but notice that the trailer landing gear was still in the up position and was too low for the tractor to get under it. I found out later that someone pulled the pin that kept the fifth-wheel jaw locked around the kingpin that normally would keep the tractor-trailer together; a dirty trick that a childish trucker would play on someone, thinking that it is all in fun! I was told about this in tractor-trailer school, and there I had seen it for myself. From that day forward, I always take the time to look under my truck when I leave it and return… just in case. That is just some of the things that I have seen out here on the road. It is a whole different world out here! After completing this tour and returning to Rochester, New York, home, it was time off for about three days.

Chapter 6

Boy's town.

Little did I know, this would be the last trip that Captain Tee would be riding with me! We were somewhere in Missouri as we were leaving I-57 and getting on I-55. I was just waking up, and Tom was driving. I told him that I had to urinate, so when he found a spot to stop, I would appreciate it. So, on the on ramp, before we entered traffic, he pulled over to the side, off the ramp, I got out and did my business and got back into the truck, and Tom started to drive, continuing to the route. As we were about to enter traffic, another truck came around the ramp and must have not seen us or missed interpreted our speed or location because the truck hit us right in the back so hard that my head was snatched back, and Tom let out a screech that sounded like he thought that this was the end for him. I remember turning to look at Tom, and I saw in the driver's mirror the objected of the disturbance; the other truck was on fire and was starting to roll to the right side of the road. I told Tom that we were hit by another truck. Tom said, "Huh?" I told him that the truck that hit us was on fire. Tom again said, "Huh?" I said, "Let's see if we can help." We got out of the truck and ran quickly back to see what could be done. The driver in the truck that was on fire said, "Please do not let me burn up in here. I pulled at the door, but it would not open." It was jammed because of the crash. Tom and a bystander worked on the driver's side front window, and we finally got the driver out and away from the truck to safety. By then, a police officer showed up and took charge of the scene. Later, an ambulance got there and found that Tom had some glass in his eyes and had him and the driver of the other truck go with them to get checked out. I, on the other hand, was left in charge of the truck. I called the dispatch to let them know about the events. The dispatch told me where to take the truck so that I could have the load transferred to another trailer and then continue the trip to Laredo, Texas. I had a load of windshield wiper motors. And so, I started my solo driving! When I arrived in Laredo on January 27, 1986, I got unloaded, and by then, the dispatch told me I would have to wait to see when they would get me another load; that was cool with me! I needed some sleep anyway, so I went to a little truck stop I found; a Phillips 66; it was a little hole-in-the-wall parking lot with a bar and a restaurant. I got a bite to eat and went back to the truck to watch some TV and fell asleep. When I woke up, the TV was a buzz with the news of the Space Shuttle Challenger disaster! They said that the Space Shuttle Challenger broke apart 73 seconds into its flight, killing all seven crew members aboard. I put on some clothes and went to the truck stop to wash up and get something to eat; everyone was talking about the shuttle disaster, and someone mentioned that one of the astronauts was a teacher; she was to be the first teacher to go into space, and there was also a Black astronaut by the name of Ronald McNair. Later that day, I went across the bridge into Mexico. Someone told me about a place in Mexico called Boys town. They told me that I could catch a local Taxi and they would take me right to it. As I remember, it was the cab driver himself that told me about it! A couple of guys took the cab with me as we headed into a deeper part of Mexico to see this Boys Town. I wondered how I would get back, and then the driver of the taxi said that he would be going to town and coming back all night. In Boys Town, there were some bars lined up like in the cowboy movies, so we picked one and went in. When we got into the little bar, I asked for a beer, and the barmaid brought me a Corona, so I tried it and found that I liked it, so I drank a few and looked at the young ladies walking around. They were looking so fine. I was separated from my wife at the time, and I was on my own. I had been on the road for a while and was starting to feel like I would like the company, so when one of the barmaids came back around to me, I asked her what her name was; she did not speak English very well, nor did I speak Spanish too well myself, but with a word here and a word there, we managed to have a conversation. She asked me if I wanted to get with her. Now, I am not one to pay for sex but, I was not in America, and she was so fine; besides, who will ever know. I asked her what it would cost me, and she said, "Not much, just five dollars American." I was pleasantly surprised and almost tore my pocket off, reaching for the five dollars and asked, "Where do we do this?" And she said, "We could get a room for seven dollars." That is still only twelve dollars, so why not? The room was like a hotel with a tub and a bed; very comfortable. We got in the bed, I started caressing her body, and she felt as good as she looked; nicely put together, soft, and she smelled good too. Before I knew it, I was so turned on that I didn't even care where I was; I just wanted her and she was going along with it, as if we were lovers all along like we knew each other for years. I wondered where she had been all my life. When I penetrated her womanhood and we became one, I felt as if we were meant to be, as if I'd found where I was supposed to be, and I didn't want this to end. But then I released the pressure that was building up in me from the time of my first penetration of her beautiful body, and I thought I was about to lose my mind at that moment. She was my world. Then she said, "You through?" I felt bad then because she did not experience it the way I did; it was just a job to her. So, I said yes, and asked where I could get washed up. When she showed me the shower, I quickly found out that there was no hot water in the hotel; the water was all cold, very cold, but I got in it and started washing up. The water was so cold that it was making me make all kinds of faces, and that made her laugh! That was not the only time something like that happened with me out there on the road. I found myself out there just going wild! There were many more trips to Mexico and other places where I enjoyed more than the scenery! While in Mexico, I was able to get my hands on some good smoke. I smoked a lot back in those days. You might say that I was a real Pot Head back then. One day when I was leaving El Paso, I stopped at a truck stop and got on the CB, and located some smoke from this driver who looked a lot like Lee Majors from the Big Valley and The Six Million Dollar Man. He said that I could come to his truck to sample it, so I did. While I was smoking, another driver contacted him and came over too. Before I knew it, we were having a real smoke party going on. By then, I was feeling the effects of the smoke, and I had to get ready to go. So, I went back to my truck and started to get to work. But as I was starting to drive off from the truck stop, I felt like I was under water; my focus was like I was looking through a bubble. I then decided that I would park and take a quick nap before making my move!

Chapter 7

Crank.

After a while, I was functional again. So, I rolled up a couple of joints and started driving. Before I got to the Pecos, I lit up a joint and rolled on down the road thinking to myself, *how great it is to be out here on my own with no one looking over my shoulders and telling me what to do!* I was free for the first time in my life. All I had to do was stay safe, legal, and make my appointments! *What a life, this is what being free is all about!* One day after I had driven a long time and I could no longer fix my logbook, I stopped at a truck stop in Ohio. I made friends with another driver and found out that he was on a break too, so we started smoking and talking. He said one thing that kind of made me wonder if he was all there! The dude said he was driving one day, and every time he got ready to pass this one car, the car kept speeding up and then slowed down again, over and over! So, he said that he moved closer to the car as if he didn't see it and snatched his tractor back so that his trailer would slap the car off the road! I wondered if he was joking that he had really knock someone off the road, but he did not crack a smile! I thought to myself, *this guy is crazy or something!* I was thinking about how I was going to get rid of him when he asked me if I wanted to try some nose candy. I then asked him what it was, and he said crank! I still was not sure what he was talking about. So, he went on to say that Crank was like coke, but it lasted longer and cost less! He let me try some. And when I did, I felt as if I had sniffed water up my nose, and I was burned like you wouldn't believe. Then, I did not want to leave out the other nostril, so I did that one too and got the same effect: burning, like I was in a pool drowning or something. He said the burning would subside shortly, and then the high would set in. He was not wrong. My nostrils started to drain, and then the buzz began. I was ready to drive some more, but I was out of legal driving time. And he said that he had a fix for that. I asked him, "What?" and he just said two words, "Back log!" "Back log?" I asked. He said, "Yes, back log!" He then said, "Fix your log so that it looks like you are legal to drive again!" I showed him my logbook and asked, "How do I do that?" He looked at my log, then said that I would need to get another logbook and start from right now, saying that I was just finishing my 10-hour sleeper birth time. This guy was a real outlaw and, I believe, a bad influence on me, but I did it and was back on the road. Being out there on the road was a different world altogether; it was like sitting on a sofa with the windshield for a movie screen. You see so much, and not the same thing all the time either. One time, as I was driving, I came upon what looked like the side of a barn beside the road, but as I got near it, I realized that it was the bottom of a truck; it was laying on its side, a reck, and I couldn't see the name on the side of the truck, but it made me see that it could've been me. I wondered what happened. I knew sometimes it can get really exhausted out there on the road, (it has happened to me many times), but I had been lucky enough to find somewhere to rest before I ended up off on the side of the road somewhere, laying on my side.

Chapter 8

Commercial Beavers.

I remember one time coming out of Texas, I got so sleepy that I nodded off to sleep for what seemed like a second or two, but I covered a lot of ground. I went from Texarkana, Texas, to Hope, Arkansas, before I knew it and was coming upon a weight scale. As I was waking up, I thought I saw a figure in the passenger seat holding the steering wheel, but I could not focus on the person, or whatever it was. It just stayed right out of site so that I could not focus on it. And the more I tried to see it, the more difficult it became to see until I came back to my senses and realized I needed to slow down to cross the scale. I made it across without a problem, but after that, I stayed awake until I found a place to get some sleep. So, I can understand how someone can get that tired. After a while, I decided to get some sleep and parked at a TA truck stop. As I was parking, the CB was a buzz! Drivers were calling out for commercial beavers (truck stop prostitutes), and a couple responded. One called Brown Sugar and another one by the name of Black Snapper. Black Snapper came to my truck and asked me if I wanted any company; I told her no. But I could not help but feel like I should have said yes, or at the very least, maybe. I was going to be there for a while, and I was alone. Then, she asked me if she could use my radio, and I said yes, giving me time to see if I would change my mind and give in to my lust or stick to my guns and go to sleep. She was not a bad-looking girl, arousing my interest and my lustful mood. When she got on the radio, she called for Brown Sugar; things were about to get real. Just as I had hoped, she had Brown Sugar come over to my truck too! When Brown Sugar got there, I noticed that she was a cutie; she was just a little taller than Black Snapper. Both had nice shapes and looked clean. And I found myself caught between two thoughts like in the cartoons, where you have an angel on one shoulder and a devil on the other! But I was cool and just talked to them as friends. it was my first time having a conversation with two truck stop commercial beavers alone in my truck! It was an experience, and I must say: I liked it! They told me that this was not the only truck stop they worked in and that they lived in the area. As we talked, I kept looking them up and down and enjoying the view. But by then, I knew that nothing lustful was going to happen, and they also realized that too. It was time to move on. We said our goodbyes. As I watched them leave my truck, I felt as though I was leaving friends, not knowing if I would see them again, but I wanted to. I went to the sleeper birth for some needed sleep, though I had Brown Sugar and Black Snapper on my mind until I went to sleep. When I finally woke up, it was six o'clock. I looked out the window of my truck. It was a sunny day, warm with no rain and a few clouds. But overall, a good day! I put on some clothes and went up to the truck stop to get cleaned up and something to eat. At the truck stop, there was a diner where you could smell the food cooking! I looked at the cart du jour (menu), and I decided to get the buffet! At the buffet, they had pancakes, sausages, eggs, biscuits, and some grits. Well, I knew right then just what I wanted… grits, eggs, and sausages with some pancakes on the side, a cup of coffee, and a glass of orange juice! And if that was not enough, I would do it all over again! When the server offered me another cup, I told her, "No thanks, if I have anymore, I would be too jittery to drive." She laughed at that. I tipped her and took off. I stopped by the truck stop store. In the store, I saw TVs, CB radios, clothes, and food. I bought some candy, a soft drink, and a couple of country music tapes: Willie Nelson's tape with the song *On the Road Again*, Jerry Reed's song from Smokey and the Bandit, and the song from Waylon Jennings and Hank Williams Jr, *The Conversation* and *Went on My Way*. When I got back to my truck, I heard drivers on the CB asking about Smoking Dope, Nose Candy, Go fast, and Commercial Beavers. Then someone answered, "Smoking dope; go to channel 15." So, I put my CB on channel 15 and listened for a bit. On channel 15, I heard a driver say that he was looking for some smoking dope; the other voice said, "I got the smoking dope; how much are you looking for?" The driver asked, "How much?" He said that he had $20.00 ounces and pounds for $100.00! The driver then asked, "Where are you?" And he said that he was on party row, that's where all the party truckers go to hide out and just have fun, and where I was parked too. He said that he was on the scales side! Then he asked the driver, "Do you see my four ways flashing?" The other driver said he did; he told him to come on over. I told him that I would like an ounce too, and I was invited over as well! When I got there, I saw that that dude had a Peterbilt long-nose truck with a walk-in sleeper! Clean as the board of health too! He let us try the smoke; it felt like we were having a party in his truck! We were passing joints around and telling jokes, listening to the CB, and just having a grand old time. I liked the smoke, so I bought an ounce and headed back to my truck! Back at my truck, I rolled up a couple of joints, started my logbook, and took off down the road. I was still listening to the CB as I drove away. Soon, the voices got so far away that I could hardly hear them at all. But other voices were coming over the CB saying things like, "There is a bear, eastbound, on eighty, at Mile Marker one zero four over three!" Then another voice said, "He made a flip and turned on his red's." I thought to myself, *Wait, I am headed eastbound on eighty!* Then in my driver's side mirror, I saw him. It was a state trooper, and he was headed my way! I took a quick look at my speed; I was doing sixty-two in a sixty-five-mph zone! About that time, the trooper passed me, and he was moving fast after that; about three more troopers zipped passed me with their red lights on too! I wondered what might be going on; a few minutes later, a fire truck and two more troopers with red lights flashing passed me, headed in the same direction at a high rate of speed! That really got me wondering. Soon they were out of sight. Everything went smooth for a while, but then, all traffic was coming to a slow down, and I could see smoke ahead of us. After a little bit, the traffic stopped altogether. I still could not see what was going on, but the CB was all a buzz with chatter about what it might be! Drivers on the westbound side said that it was a big accident; two tractor-trailers and some cars were involved, traffic was backed up for two to three miles, and no lanes were open! I was to sit there for I don't know how long now! I heard some drivers talking, and one of them said he knew a way around the backup. He said to just get off at the next exit and go south for about a quarter of a mile, then turn right at the second stop sign, and follow that for about twelve miles, then make another right and go through a small town, and you would run right back into I-80 West. So, at the next exit, I saw some trucks getting off the interstate; I got off too! There were about four trucks ahead of me, and I could see some more joining the line-up behind me! I listened in on the CB as I went along. Soon, I found myself getting back on I-80 Eastbound! I still do not know what happened at that accident. But I was back on track now. By now, I was in Chicago, where I was to pick up my load. I stopped at a truck stop to relieve myself and to get something to eat. And then on to my stop! At my destination, I saw a building that looked like a big office building; I looked for a dock, but I did not see one. So, I asked someone, and I was led to a big door in the side of the building and was told that I had to go in that way. So, I started driving into it! It was like driving down a hallway at a school. Inside, the walls were kind of tight and the ceiling was high enough for the truck, but it still seemed weird driving inside of a building. I then noticed a sign directing me to a section of the building with an opening and a right turn in the center. A tight right turn at that! I thought that it was an impossibility, but I made it safely. I then saw an opening in the middle of the building; it was like a courtyard, surrounded by four walls... only the sky above for a rooftop. To my right, I could see the docks; I backed up to one and went to talk to the shipper about the load information. There were three other drivers from my company there. We talked while we were being loaded. We found out that we were not going to the same place with our load; we could ride together for a little while on this trip, though. They were headed to Laredo, Texas, but I was headed to Oklahoma. As soon as the last of us was loaded, we started the run. We left the city and headed south on I-57. Our first break was in St. Louis, Illinois; I just had to get to see St. Louis Arch! I went all the way up in the arch and looked out over the river; it felt like the arch was swaying in the breeze; it felt unnerving! But I enjoyed it anyway. When I looked down, I noticed a couple of river boats from which you could take a tour of the river. So, I went down and got on one. It took me down the river a bit, and it reminded me of the ones that you would see in the old movies, like Tom Sawyer, where you have the big paddle on the back, the water being parted by the front of the boat, and the soothing sound of the old Mississippi River. I liked that I could see parts of the United States that I had only heard about as a kid, read about in books, or looked at on television. As the boat began to turn around, I noticed a riverboat that was a gambling casino docked at the shore, and people were milling around all over it and the dock. But it was time for me to get some sleep. So, when I returned to my truck, I climbed back in the birth and went to sleep. Later, when I got up, I started my logbook and got going. I went west on I-44, and I was again on my way. The next place of interest was Oklahoma. I passed through Springfield and Joplin, Missouri, on the way to Oklahoma and went by the Cherokee Nation. I also went in between Tulsa and Broken Arrow, Oklahoma. I saw a sign that said Muscogee Creek Nation; then I came to Oklahoma City, where I got off I-44 and got onto I-35 South. I passed through the Chickasaw Nation and then into Marietta, Oklahoma. To unload after that, I went to Denton, Texas, where I picked up another load. This one was going to Laredo, Texas. I took I-35 South on the east side and through Dallas, Texas. When I got to Laredo, it was too late to get unloaded. So, I went to the Phillip sixty-six truck stop. This truck stop was in such bad shape that the driveway and the parking lot were dirt! And it had so many large holes filled with water from the rain. I ran in one that was so big that I could swear I heard another truck driver down there asking me if I knew the way up out of here! I was wondering if it was going to break the truck's axles. I got parked and went to the truck stop. I was the only Black guy there! I met two other drivers, and we introduced ourselves to each other. We were from the same company. Then we joked about the shape the truck stop was in and had a few beers. We started playing some pool, talking, sharing truck driver stories, and telling jokes. Then another guy came into the truck stop's bar where we were playing pool. He was a young white guy; he had on a cowboy hat, a vest, blue jeans with the cuff turned up, and cowboy boots. The boots were a light color and looked like they were made from snakeskin or something. He came over and put his quarters on the table and calmly said, next! Then went over to the bar and got a beer. He reminded me of the young gunfighters who walked into the bar in old western movies. So, when it was his turn to play, he came over to the table. Since I won the last game, he had to play me. I broke the balls, and nothing fell, so it was his shot. As he lined up for a shot, he stepped on one of my boots; I thought to myself, *let me move over out the way.* I was also thinking to myself, *he could say excuse me or something.* He made his shot and set up for the next one and stepped on my boot again; well, I thought to myself, *this guy is doing this on purpose*, so I said, "Can you watch your step? You are stepping on my boots!" The whole room got quiet; you could have heard a pen drop! Everybody in the room looked our way; there were only Mexicans and Whites in the bar, heck, in the whole town as far as I knew. Then the cowboy said, "Excuse me and moved over. Then when it was his time to shoot again, he walked over to where I was, and the room got quiet again, and he leaned over to speak to me and said, in a soft tone, "Let me know if I get crooked." Then he walked over to the other side of the table and started to line up his shot. I couldn't help but think it was funny when he was lining up his shot, and one side of his hip was offset, like when you would be getting on a bike! I realized that he was making a joke, and I said, "You are getting crooked!" And everybody started to laugh; everything worked out. After that, the other guys that were from my company and I got a bite to eat; then, we produced the idea of going across the border for some fun. After that, we went back to our trucks, and I went to bed for the night. Not long after that trip, I left that company and started working for a local company: E.L. Lawson Trucking. It was a Black-owned company, and it had mostly all Black drivers. And I was back to driving as a team again. On my first trip with this company, it was one that I knew oh so well; it was Laredo, Texas. When the owner told me about it, I remember asking him, "Was the address on Scott Street?" He looked at me inquisitively and said, "Yes," and continued, "have you been there before?" I let him know that the other company I was with sent me there a lot. So, we got ready for the trip. We started out by going to pick up the load; it was a place right there in town. We were picking up GM products and windshield wiper motors. Spud was the driver I was to team up with, and once we were loaded up, we drove from Mount Reed Boulevard south to four ninety west to I-90 West. Spud went into the sleeper birth to get some sleep while I had the Helm. We were supposed to be driving in eight-hour shifts, but after my shift, I was still wide awake! I was too excited to get to sleep. When Spud got up, I was headed into Cincinnati, Ohio. He asked me if I was all right, and I told him that I was good! Then he asked me if I was ready to change places yet. I told him I could go some more. He sat up with me for a while, and we talked and road until it was time to get some fuel. So, we stopped at a truck stop, and fueled up, got something to eat, used the bathroom, and then got back on the road.

Chapter 9

Coolaid!

When I finally got tired, we were coming into a city in Tennessee called Brownsville; that is where we stopped, fueled up, got something to eat, and took a shower. After that, I was ready for some sleep! I crawled into the sleeper birth. I was sleeping so well until I felt the truck stopping fast; I wondered what was going on. Spud said that he had to make a quick stop; well, that suited me fine! I needed to stop too! Bathroom time. After that, we were on our way again. We decided that when we got past the weight scale, we were going to roll up a joint apiece and ride high for a while. Before I started working at this company, I had already changed my handle from Black Cowboy to Kool-Aid, but after so many people tried to be funny by asking me what flavor, I changed the K to a C and changed the meaning also! I started saying it is not Kool-Aid with a K, But Cool Aid with a C, because it is not the drink but an attitude adjustment; when you are sad, I will try to bring you a smile. I try to help your cool. I try to *Aid Your Cool.* The young lady that I was dating at the time I was going to tractor-trailer school, who also introduced me to her friend who told me about how to get a grant, had a daughter that said that she was going to start calling me Kool-Aid because when she would get home from school, I would have finished all the Kool-Aid before she got home all the time! So, when I was ready to change my handle, I felt that it would fit my personality very well! So that's how spud would address me when he was trying to get my attention. Although Spud was younger than I was, he taught me a lot of tricks of the trade. We made friends fast because we had a lot in common. I thought he was cool. When we finished the run and got back to the terminal, we were sent right back out to do it all over again. When we finished that run, I was put with another driver. His handle was Trouble Man, and we were headed to Tuscaloosa, Alabama. As we road, we talked, and I found out that back in the 60s, a lady that I was with a few times was an ex-wife of his! I thought that this could get awkward, but he said that she was a mistake and that they divorced a long time ago. After a while, the awkwardness subsided, and we became friends and were able to carry on. When we got that run out the way and got back home, I was handed a considerable sum of money (cash)! And I was well pleased! I took the weekend off. And then I was back at it again! This time, with another driver. His handle was Ever Ready! You know, like the batteries. He was a cool number two; he took a lot of back roads and knew all the neighborhood truck stops, where there were people like me, with foods that I liked to eat and foods that I grew up on. Yeah, I knew I was going to like that! I needed to remember some of those places for when I am out there on my own, by myself, or just traveling in my personal vehicle. We continued the route until we got to Texarkana, Arkansas, where we took Highway 59 south. I have never been on that route before, and it made the trip more interesting! We stayed on 59 until we reached Houston, where we got on I-10 and headed west all the way to San Antonio. There, we took I-35 South into Laredo. When we left Laredo, we stopped in Stuttgart, Arkansas, at Riceland Rice, for a load of rice for our back-haul. Stuttgart is a nice little country town. It reminds me of my hometown in Florida. There were some other trucks there to get loaded too! There was a little restaurant on site where we grabbed some breakfast. Then we picked up our load and delivered it. I remember another time when I was on the run; I was riding with Trouble Man, coming through Ohio. It was two of our trucks and a flatbed truck from another company running together. When the flatbed truck started to make his pass, he looked over at our truck and made out like he wanted to race. Trouble Man took the bait and started to speed up increasingly. After a while, our trucks were doing about 90 mph and still speeding up. The flatbed truck started to slow down; I guess he did not want to go any faster. These were tractor-trailers, and it would be hard to stop them if we had to. Yeah, I know, it was extremely dangerous! But it was also overly exciting. It was a real rush! But that was not the only exciting thing I got into. Once while Trouble Man and I were on the run and it was my turn to drive, we switched places at 70 mph. Then he told me to take the wheel, so I put one hand on the wheel as he let go of the wheel, and he began to slide out of the seat, and I slid into it; without stopping or even slowing down. That was wild, crazy, and dangerous! But that was some of the stuff you do when you are young and not fearful of what could happen. But everything turned out ok. I road with some other drivers in this company too. One of them went by the name of Houdini! The first place we went to was Parlin, New Jersey, and from there, we went to Clifton, New Jersey. And return. Next, we went to Tuscaloosa, Alabama, and Des Plaines, Illinois. Also, me and another driver named Cameo ran together for a while; we went to Laredo, Texas, and Sioux City, Iowa, and some other places too. And then there was the owner's brother-in-law; his handle was Mandingo! And another driver named Milton; I do not know what his handle was. I stayed with this company for about a year or so; then, I decided to move on. I went back to Ryder again. This time, the trucks were not like the ones I was driving when I was with them before. They had old, one-stack Mack's with a window in the back, ten-speed transmissions, and a long hood in front. I also met some new drivers. We went to some unfamiliar places; we were going over to Liverpool, New York, at the time; to a warehouse. We were still going to Hamlin and Brockport. After apple season was over, I collected unemployment for a while.

Then, I went back to Lawson Trucking; the owner's son said that if I left again, they would not hire me back; I just said *OK!* During the time I had worked with this company, I picked up quite a few speeding tickets… *who would have thought?!* One day, as I was returning from a run to Laredo, I called home for a ride. I was told by my girlfriend's daughter that her mother was in the hospital. I asked her, "Is she having the baby now?" And she said, "Yes!" I got home as quickly as possible, washed up, changed clothes, and headed to the hospital in my girlfriend's car. I was driving as fast as I could, taking 45 mph curves at 60 mph! I also stopped at red lights just long enough to see if anyone was coming and then sped through them until I made it to the hospital. Luckily, I made it safely and without getting any tickets. I got to the delivery room at about 3:15; I got there just in time because, at 3:30, she gave birth to my son, and I was right there to welcome him into this world. I was holding my girlfriend's right leg as she gave birth, and from where I was positioned, I was the first to see that he was a boy. When I went back to work, I was told that they could no longer insure me because of all the tickets I picked up over the time that I had been driving. I was out of a job with a newborn son! So, now I had to find another job! I tried custodial work, plastic mold injection, and even went to tool and die school and got a job in tool and die. I did that for about six months or so; then, I was fired from that job because I made too many mistakes. After that, it seemed like I could not find a job anywhere! Things got so bad that my girlfriend broke up with me while I was still living with her! We walked around in the same house with little to say to each other! I felt like everything I said irritated her!

Chapter 10

A change in my life.

One day I was out of cigarettes. I asked my son's mother for one of hers; she sat back on the couch, crossed her legs, and handed me the pack like I was a begging peasant. And there were times that when we were going to bed that we would go upstairs to get into bed, and she would go back downstairs. To keep her company, I would go back too, and again she would go back upstairs; then it struck me that she was trying to put space in between us! I felt so low and sad that I just sat downstairs with tears in my eyes and wondered what was next; *what do I do now?* I had a son, no job, and my girlfriend was fed up with me! I was as low as I could go. I felt like I had given up. My life was messed up! I had hit rock bottom! The television was on, and I heard a preacher talking, and he was making a lot of sense!! Then one thing he said got my attention. He said that making a vow to God and keeping it would be stepping out on faith, showing that you believe in God and that HE is a rewarder of those who seek HIM diligently. And I was at that time totally convinced that those words were true. So, I found a quiet place in the apartment, the bathroom, and started to pray and cry out for God to hear my plea. I asked God to save me now or just take me away because I had ruined my life, and I did not know what else to do. I was already going to church on Sundays! But now, even that became more real than ever before; I was playing or trying to play guitar in church and sitting up front, in the front row; Amen corner! Then one day... A day came that I had to leave. Not because I was trying to dump her, but because she wanted me to go. I did not break up with her; she broke up with me. Having no money, no job, and nowhere to go, I went to my mother's house. After about a month, I was able to find a job driving again. I started working for a place called Staub Textile Services. It started with a phone call from Ryder Truck Rental; I was told that I was next in line on a list that I did not even know that I was still on, seeing that I had been out of contact with Ryder for about maybe four years! They said that there was a company that wanted me to fill in for another driver who was out sick; I was to fill in for the holidays, which I said yes to. But before December was over, I kept hearing something in my heart saying that they were going to give me this job. But I kept saying in my heart that I would not want to take someone's job like that!! Then in the last part of December, I was told that I would be there at least until after the New Year; I said no problem. one day, I said, "LORD, if this is the job that you want me to have: then you will be done!" The job was easy; I would get to work at around four in the evening and check to see what trailer was loaded. There were two to pick from: one going to Syracuse and the other to Buffalo. Sometimes I would go to Syracuse first. With that one being the first one, I would pre-trip the rig and then go on my way. Going out of the gate and making a right turn, I would head east on Main Street to Culver Road, make another right, and then left to get on 490 east and take that to I-90 East. The directions they gave me said to take I-90 east to exit 35 and then go around the traffic circle to the third exit, which will be Thompson Road. I then would go past the carrier auto plant, and at the second light, make a left, and then a quick right into the parking lot, go around the building to the back; the dock would be the second one down on my left. When I got ready to back up, I got out to open the trailer doors and backed up to the dock to unload. The load was strapped in; I had to unstrap it. It had metal crates with wheels, and they were loaded with clean clothes and rugs; I would just roll them off the truck and push the other ones on, strap them down and close the trailer doors. Then, I was on my way back to Rochester. Back at Rochester, I would drop that trailer and hook it to the other one and take off for Buffalo. Turning left out of the job this time and onto Main Street, this time heading westbound to the inter loop westbound and on to 490 west to I-90 west towards Buffalo. After a while, I started meeting with some of the people who were working in the toll booths. A lot of them were females; one such female was a young lady; she said that her name was Jan. I introduced myself, but by now, other vehicles were piling up behind me at the toll booth, so I said that I would see her later and went on my way. In Buffalo, as I was turning into the driveway, I passed a pizza shop. I decided that after I got done here, I would stop in for a bite. When I got into the shop, I looked at the menu. They had tacos, both soft and crispy shells, dessert pizzas, and diverse types of soft drinks, including one that I had never heard of… Loganberries. So, I ordered a soft-shell taco with sour cream, a cherry cheesecake pizza, and a large loganberry drink to go. When I got back to my truck, I opened the bag to see one of the biggest tacos I had ever seen, a soft taco that looked like a burrito, and it was the size of my wrist! And from bite one to the last, it was delicious. And the loganberry drink… man; it tasted like a juice, not carbonated. I now had a new favorite drink; I loved it! The cherry cheesecake pizza was out of this world! I was going to put on too much weight coming to this place every day! When I finished, I was so full that I just had to take a little nap; good thing it was the last run for the night. Sometimes, while coming over there or to Syracuse, I would stop at one of the service plazas on the way and take a thirty-minute nap. Other times, I would stop by a service plaza for a bite to eat, a bathroom break, and a nap. The first time I stopped there, they had a program called Road Warrior in which a truck driver would get a discount on their order; there was even a card you could get to show that you were a truck driver. If you showed them your license to sign up, the card would come in the mail in about a week or so. It was sponsored by the Marriott. And other times, on the way back from Syracuse, I would stop at a rest area on the road and listen to a program on the radio called Unshackled, a dramatized story about people coming to know Jesus Christ; some were a lot like my story. It stayed on for about half an hour; sometimes, I would be at so much peace that I would fall to sleep to be awakened by the theme music and the announcement of the end of the show. Time to roll on and head for home. This program became a part of my life; sometimes, I could find it on other radio stations and listen to it two to three times a night. Some of the programs were biblical teachings and some Bible readings. I was learning so much about the Bible and biblical theology. I got to the place where I would even pray in the truck before I started each run. One day while I was praying, a young lady saw me and said that she caught me sleeping; I let her know that I was praying, not sleeping as she thought. I was enjoying this job! I was at peace, and I had my alone time! And not only that, but it seemed as though every couple of months or so, I was getting an increase in pay! Early one morning after work, I would be on my way home and thought to myself how I would like to have someone to talk to and start a relationship with. When I spotted a young lady on the way, she looked like, just maybe, she might be the one. I was once into the wildlife, and the word of God reached me and brought me out of that lifestyle; I believed it would do the same for her. This could be the one for me. She waved me down, so I stopped to see what she wanted. She asked me if I would give her a ride to her house; I was pleased that she asked, and I was also pleased that I quickly said that I would; when she got in the car, I could not help but notice that she really did not look bad. In fact, she looked physically attractive. She asked me where I was coming from this time of night. I told her that I was just finishing work for the night and was headed home to go to bed. She asked me about my job; I told her that I was a truck driver and that I did the night shift. I also told her that I got to work at six to whatever time I finished, and I did not have to clock in or out because I got paid by the job, not by the hour. As we turned on her street, I saw her hand reaching out towards my right thigh, and just as she touched me, I blurted out I am saved! At that, she stopped her move. I was wondering to myself, *where did that come from?* It just popped out of my mouth unexpectedly! And then she said that no one would know! And just as unexpectedly as the words that came out of my mouth the first time, I heard myself saying, but GOD knows! She stopped again, and I was really wondering what was going on. I wanted to get with her, and she was making the first move, but I just could not go on with it; something within me kept stopping me! I asked her why she would put herself out there like that. I told her that I thought she could be with someone who wanted her for more than a trick, that she would be a prime candidate for someone as a wife, and that she might even be the person God has made just for me. At that, she decided to leave the vehicle. I thought to myself, you must be crazy; she was in your car and ready to do the do, and you talked her out of it! I mentally beat myself up all the way home. She was the first woman to get in my car since I got it. It was not a bad-looking car, a 1979 Lincoln Continental, all white. Anyway, I went home, showered, and went to bed. I watched television until I fell asleep. I slept until it was time to go back to work. Not too long after I started working with this company, they gave me a cellphone; it was big and looked like one of those G.I. Joe telephones, only smaller. I remember one time being on my mother's back porch and calling her with that cellphone. When she answered her phone, I said, "Hey moms, guess where I am?" She asked, "Where?" And I said with joy; I am on the back porch! She replied, "Where?" I laughed and repeated on the back porch! We both got a good laugh out of that. But then the day came that I received the phone bill... it was so high that I thought about giving the phone back to the people that I had gotten it from! But I kept it. It came in very handy. One night while on the highway headed to Syracuse, I stopped at a service plaza for a bite. As I was sitting in the truck while eating, I was listening to a Bible reading show that made me question myself! Am I really born again, or am I just going along with what was being said? So, I turned off the radio and started to pray with all that was in me. Saying to God, "Lord, I repent of my sin, and I give full control of my life to you. For YOU are the only God that I know from my grandmother's teaching and the way she lived her life! I know that your words are true, and I want to live by them and follow you all the days of my life! In the name of Jesus Christ, your only begotten son, Amen. Then I continued to Syracuse. I was starting to get back into working out, too. You see, I was noticing that my stomach was really starting to stick out too much, so it was time to do something about it! I would do jumping jacks and sit-ups to get it down. I kept hearing about doing crunches from a therapist that I was going to for my back pain, so I decided to try some. I was able to do one hundred sit-ups by doing fifty at a time. So, I did that with the crunches; they were easy, not as hard as sit-ups. I did about a hundred and then switched the load. That was on a Friday, and a good thing too. On Saturday, my abdominal muscles were locked tight as the strings on a guitar! They hurt so bad that I had trouble even walking! And to laugh was unbearable that I thought I was going to cramp up. My niece kept making me laugh, and I would beg her to stop! But she kept on. I was like that for about two to three days. I realized I was working on muscles that I had never worked on before, and I did far too many of them for the first time. After a while, I got used to doing crunches, and I would do them regularly. At some of the tollbooths, I got to meet the toll operators, and we sometimes got a chance to talk. There were a couple of them I tried to foster an off-duty relationship with, but nothing came of that effort. One day, the regional manager and the general manager of the company called me into the office. I started to wonder, *what could it be about?* It was either the guy whose place I was covering for came back, or I did something wrong. But then I had that thought again; the thought came from nowhere. It said, *the job is yours.* In the office, I met with two of the managers, and we small-talked until the main manager got there. After the initial hellos and salutations, I was notified that people were watching me and that there were people who wanted my job! And then he said that he wanted to give me the first shot at it! Then he asked me straight out, "Do you want this job permanently?" But before he could even finish, I already had a big smile on my face, and I replied, "Yes, yes, I would like to have this job! And I must apologize for not showing a lot more excitement, but something in my heart had already told me that the job was mine!" They looked at each other and then at me. They looked at me like I was out of my mind. But I knew it was God all the time. I worked there from November, just before my birthday in 1991, to February 1996. Then, I felt the longing to go on the road again! I was told that I was at the top of my paygrade and there would be no more raises, no more room for improvement, and no more incentives. So, I started looking for another job, somewhere where I could advance and see more than Rochester, Buffalo, and Syracuse all the time! I wanted to travel some more.

Chapter 11

Refrigerated.

In 1997, about a year after I left Staub's Textile, I started working for a company called T.R.L. (Transcontinental Refrigerated Lines). It was in Pittston, Pennsylvania. This job was a game changer! In orientation, they went over where and how to get our paperwork into the company so that we could be paid; we had debit cards on which our pay would be deposited. I was also shown how to restart the refrigerator unit if, by chance, it got cut off or ran out of fuel! We were given some snow chains for roads that got icy, and we were given fuel cards that we could also get cash advances for tolls or personal expenses. And some other things that I was not aware of; we had to unload a lot of the times, we were allowed to hire lumpers, and the company would pay them with a com-check. And the trucks were huge! Big Freightliners: mine was a mid-roof. So, I could stand up in this one; I liked that! Lawson had some that I could stand up in too, but this one, I was by myself! I remember buying a television at a truck stop in Jacksonville, Florida, so that I would have something to do while waiting to be loaded or at my off times. One day while I was in Kansas City, I ran into someone who was selling what he called "privacy curtains." I bought a pair and put them up in my truck. That made it seem like I was in a cozy little apartment. Sometimes I could not wait to shut down; it was like being home. I had to find an antenna to pick up local television stations in whatever city I happened to be in at the time. In some places, I could pick up a lot of stations, and other times, I could not get any. And the truck radio was about the same! So, I invested in satellite radio. I still bought food from whatever was nearby, some good and some not so much. One night, while I was traveling, I was out in a secluded area, and suddenly, I heard a loud pop, and my truck started losing power; smoke was coming out of the smokestack. I did not have a phone at that time, just a pager. There was nowhere to look for a phone, so I opened the hood of my truck and looked around to see if there was anything that I could do to fix that problem. I noticed that the turbo booster had a large tube that came apart, and a clamp had broken. But there was another one there! It was like someone put two on it! I took out my pocketknife and loosened the remaining clamp; I then placed it where the tube met the turbo and clamped it down. I started the truck up again, and I did not see any smoke; the noise was gone too, so I got back into the truck and started driving, and the problem was fixed! I fixed the truck on my own! So, I continued. Getting the loads were different too! I would get a message on my pager; then, I would locate a phone to answer the page; usually, it would be the dispatcher with load information and a number to call for the rest of the information. I needed to keep a pencil and some paper on hand all the time.

In this one place they sent me, I had to pick up a load of hams from a place called Cooks! And I took the hams over to Kansas City and into a cave! There were some other trucks there also, two of them were from my company. I followed them to find out how this was going to play out, some of the other drivers were docked at outside docks, but we went inside! I was amazed at the size of the cave; there was so much room in it! It even had a rail system inside parts of it. The caves had refrigerated compartments to keep products cold. This was the first time that I had ever been in a cave, let alone driven into one! There were a lot of first times with this job. The first time I went to California was with this company! That run began in the state and town where I was living, Rochester, New York; I received the load from Kodak, a load of film bound for Hollywood, California. I traveled there in four days. On my way to California, I saw a sign that said trucks must wear chains; I was told in orientation how to chain up; they said that in certain states, it was the law when the signs were lit up. I was not sure how to do it, but I had to try! I struggled for about twenty minutes or so and only got one of them on… and then the light went off. I did not need to chain up now; I needed to take them off now! I was sweating in the snow! But at least I got them back off and went on my way. I came across a large hill called The Grapevine! On my way up the grapevine, the going was terribly slow; I thought I would never reach the top! But then I did get there, and it was a long way down. I started to smell smoke, and I saw what was called an escape ramp on the way down. I was wondering, *what if I had to use one?* I had a long way to go, and my brakes were already smoking. I did make it down, though, without a problem. In Hollywood, I saw palm tree-lined streets! I drove across them, not on them! And I tried so hard to spot at least one celebrity along the way, but I did not see one. After I got unloaded, my next dispatch was due north: Sacramento, California. There was a farm there that loaded me up; then, I was headed back east. On the way, I met another driver from the same company I was working for. He mentioned stopping over in Reno, Nevada, for a quick break. I had never been there before; I was with it! We parked our trucks in a big parking lot in Reno and got on the shuttle and went on into the Casino. There were people everywhere, and all kinds of noises coming from the gambling machines inside, and the voices of all the people, cigarette smoke, and the smell of alcohol. As the other driver was gambling, I went upstairs to watch a movie. On the way upstairs, I was looking at some of the fine young ladies walking around there. I walked around and watched some of the people gambling; then, I found a place to sit down and watched the horses race for about three or four screens at the same time! And then I tried out the buffet; I went straight for the crab legs.

After that, I was getting tired and decided to go to my truck and get some sleep. So, I caught up with the other driver and told him what I was going to do, and he said that he was going to be there for a while longer; after that, he would be ready to go! I told him to wake me up when he was ready to go. I caught the shuttle back to my truck, got in, closed the privacy curtains, and got in the bunk. When I woke up, I parted my curtains and looked out to see if the other driver had gotten back yet; he had not! I decided I better get my butt out of there and on down the road. That was the first and last time I was in Reno. There was this one time I was in Ohio on I-71, Northbound; it was a chilly day with a little snow and ice on the road. There was a tractor-trailer in front of me, and I was keeping my distance. Just then, the truck in front of me began to lose control. The trailer started to fishtail and then appeared to be about to jack-knife, but it straightened out. The cab of the truck and the trailer were now sideways, blocking both lanes. It was sliding down the highway, and I was thinking to myself, *this truck is about to turn over!* But then it straightened out, and I relaxed because I was sliding, trying to stop, and I noticed the truck kept sliding until it was facing across the road again, but this time, it turned the other way, blocking the road again. I thought that I was going to hit him because I was getting too close, but then it started to slide back into the ditch to my left, and I was able to get by safely. I got to hand it to him; he did an excellent job keeping that truck upright! There was another time I was in the same area, headed the same way. It was some time in the evening, and I was ready to get something to eat, shower, and sleep, not necessarily in that order. I was working on my third day without a shower, and I was feeling a little self-conscious. I was passing some trucks, and I heard a sweet voice on my CB radio. I passed about four trucks, and I heard the voice say, "Come on, T.R.L., let us break the law." I did not know what she was talking about. I did not know that the speed limit was 55 for trucks and 65 for cars, so I just said, "Come on!" And about four trucks followed me up the road for a while; then, at the exit for the truck stop, I got off. One truck followed me to the truck stop. It was the lady with the sweet voice. She was not bad looking herself. All the time, I was thinking to myself, *I need a shower! I cannot get close to her; I do not want her to smell me like this!* Looking at her, I could see that she liked pleasant things; her hair was freshly done, her nails were nice, and she had clean clothes; I was ashamed of myself! She said that she was going to Rochester too and we could ride together. I said that sounds good, but I need to take a shower first. She decided that she was ready to go; she had to roll. So, we parted ways, and I went to the truck stop and took a shower, got something to eat, and got in my bunk. I woke up the next morning with the events of the previous day still on my mind. I got up and went in to get breakfast and then started on my way. The next time I took a break was at home; I stayed home for about three days and then went back to the terminal. I had been promised a better truck as soon as one was available. When I got back to the terminal, I was told that one had just become available; I turned in my paperwork and was told where my new truck was to be found. When I found the truck, someone still had their stuff in it. After locating the driver whose stuff was in the truck, I told him that I was supposed to be moving into it, and he told me that he had no knowledge of that! He did not even know that he was to move out of the truck that day, and now, he had to call his wife to come to pick him up! And he was from out of town. He said that he would take his stuff out of the truck and put them in the driver's lounge until his wife got there. So, I waited for him to move his stuff, and then I moved mine in. It was like my old one; I could stand up in it because it was a mid-roof too. It was also newer. I then got my load information and headed out. This load took me into the back woods of Ohio, on some little road that made me think that I was on the wrong road! It did not look like it was built for big trucks. It was a dirt road that went so far back that I started to sweat; I could see what looked like a lake in front of me! But before I got that far, the road made a slight right turn, and as I got into the turn, I saw the building ahead of me. After I got docked, I went in with my information. As I was being loaded, I noticed that they were loading me with toilets.

Chapter 12

On the road again.

After they were finished, I asked, "Is there another way to get out of this place?" With a snicker, I was told, "Nope. That is all you got to work with right there!" I got out safely, though. As I was on my way to my next stop, I was thinking about the guy that had this truck before me. I was thinking of how he got fired and did not even know until I came for it. I thought to myself, *that could have just as well been me!* And I lived out of state. I wouldn't have had anyone to come to pick me up. I started thinking that it was time for me to find a local job soon. So, one day, I left that job to find a local one. It wasn't long before I started another job, this time closer to home, only two exits away! And it wasn't just any old job! I would go to New York City, Boston, Pennsylvania, and New Jersey. I did not like going to New York City all the time, but every time I went to New Jersey, I would end up going to New York! One day as I was leaving New York, I made up my mind that this was going to end right now! So, when I was unloaded, I headed back to the terminal. When I got there, I was told that they had another run set up for me! I told them, "No, you do not. I am quitting as of right now!" The dispatch was surprised, but it was over! I turned in the keys, took my stuff out of the truck, and I was gone. After about four months, I took a job as a Bus Driver. I did that for one season and then went back on the road again. I got a job driving with a company called Rosedale; they had another one of their drivers pick me up on his way back down to Dalton, Georgia, where the terminal was located. I got there, and I was set up with a hotel while I was in orientation. After orientation, I was assigned a truck, and my dispatch was to get a load from Tunnel Hill, Georgia, going north to Rochester, New York. I was following another truck from the same company; his handle was Shadow Boxer; he knew the way and had been at that location before. We got loaded with carpets, and the load had so many carpets that the trailer looked like a pregnant elephant. We weighed our trucks, started our logbooks, and we were on our way! It's a good thing that we did weigh our trucks and did our logs because right away, we came up to a weight scale just before we got out of Georgia, a little before Chattanooga, Tennessee. We were traveling on I-75 North as we left Georgia and into Chattanooga; there were about three or four truck stops that we passed along the way. When we got to Knoxville, we stopped for a bite to eat. There were about four truck stops there, too; we stopped at a small one and parked. I couldn't help but notice that there was not only food in there, but also radios, televisions, and CB radios! We could take showers, buy clothes, boots, sneakers, and so on. I bought a couple of pieces of chicken and some potato wedges; I also got a coke to drink. I got tired after that, but we had to get going. The next time we stopped, we were at a place called Tom's Brook, Virginia; Shadow Boxer said that it was the halfway point, so after a shower and a meal, I crawled back into the sleeper birth. It was about nine o'clock; I watched TV for a while and then fell asleep with the TV on. At our destination in Rochester, we went around to the back of this little building where some straight trucks were parked; we talked to the guys inside about the load, then we were told to back up to the docks.

Chapter 13

Mississippi Red

We were also told that when we were in Rochester for a layover, we could park our trucks there. So, I took a couple of days off, and I started leaving my personal car there when I was working and leaving the truck there when I was home. On one trip, as Shadow Boxer and I were pulling into a truck stop in Hershey, Pennsylvania, I was headed to a fuel pump when I saw another truck that started to make its way to the lane that I was already in. But I was already there, and I was not going to let him force me to stop so that he could get to the pump. After all, I was already in the lane. So, I stopped at the pump to fuel up, and as I got out of the truck, this young lady walked in my direction, looking right in my face, with a little smile on her face. She stood about 5'5 or 5'6 and looked as though she weighed somewhere between 125 to 135. Her skin was the color of mocha, her hair was nicely kept, and she had a little bounce to her step. She walked right up to me, looked me in my eyes, and said, "Why didn't you let me get to the pump you were parked in?" Her voice was so sweet. I was pleased with the way she came up to me. I was looking into her eyes, and with a smile on my face, I told her that if I knew that it was her in that truck, I would've jumped at the opportunity to let her get ahead of me. She smiled! We continued talking and getting to know each other better, and she said that they called her Mississippi Red. I thought, *how fitting!* I told her that I was called Coolaid! She smiled again. I found her pleasant to be around, so I asked her where she was headed. We were going in the same direction for a while, so she, Shadow Boxer, and I fueled up, picked up some snacks and something to drink, then set out on our way. As we rode Mississippi Red, I kept up our conversation. I told her where I was from, and she said that she was from Gulfport, Mississippi, and she worked for a company called Fastway Transportation. She also told me that she was originally from Brooklyn, New York and that she was of Spanish background; she told me she was alone because of the over-the-road job. I explained that I could understand that because I was having problems with home life too, and that, for right now, I did not have anyone either. I told her that it would be nice to have a mate who drove trucks also! I asked her if she would like to team up with me and drive for the same company. She said that she did not want to leave her company. I then thought to myself, *maybe if I would work for her company, it just might work out.* I was wondering, *if we did hook up as team drivers, would we ever get any work done?* I started asking questions that I figured would make or break the deal, and she asked me some too. Everything was good, and it sounded like it was going to work out. We talked about a lot of things, even about the Bible. I was still thinking about us working as a team, but with what company? I liked the truck I was driving, but I did not mind spending some off time in Gulfport, Mississippi, from time to time, hanging around the beaches and not being far away from New Orleans. I liked New Orleans when I was there before, but it would be more fun with someone at my side, and she fit the bill!   As we were coming into New Jersey, we approached a tollbooth, and Shadow Boxer went in one, and Mississippi Red was headed in another. I was following Shadow Boxer, and just before I got in the toll, Mississippi Red changed her mind and started to switch lanes. Everyone was slowing down and stopping to let her into the lane she wanted. As we cleared the toll, we came to a point where we were going separate ways. She got off at the first exit, but me and Shadow Boxer kept driving. And that was the last time I saw or heard from Mississippi Red; I did not get her phone number, so I could not contact her or anything! It was for the best, I guess.

Chapter 14

R.V.A. Trucking

This was a local job! It was in construction, hauling construction materials for companies doing roadways, parking lots, and buildings. I drove dump trucks and some tractor-trailers. I even was tested on eight, ten, and thirteen-speed transmission, and I passed the test and got the job. When I arrived at the rock quarry, I had to stop on a scale to be weighed, then I spoke with the loader driver about where to drop off the load, and then I returned to the scale to pick up my scale ticket and headed back to get another load. One day, I was put into a better truck, a Mack; it was more comfortable and less noisy! I could play the radio, and it had a ten-speed transmission. We went out one day to load asphalt; I followed another driver to learn about the process of this new endeavor. I was told to soak down the truck's box so that the asphalt wouldn't stick, and it would empty easily, and then how to tarp the load after loading so that it didn't get too cold before we got it unloaded. They tested me on some old trucks: Brockway's and Mack's. These trucks had two stick shifters in them; one had a high-low stick with a five-speed, and the other had a five-speed and a four-speed stick. I noticed that with a load, it was harder to stop, so I had to start stopping sooner just to be on the safe side! I found out the hard way one day! I was loaded, coming down a hill, and the light ahead of me turned red! I was trying to stop, but the truck did not slow down at all! I was standing up on the brakes; it slowed down but still did not stop! I was beginning to go through the light, and cross traffic was headed out. All I could do was make a right turn to keep from hitting oncoming traffic! I had slowed down enough to turn but not enough to stop. My heart was pounding at this point. From that time on, I realized that you had to be on your toes when driving a loaded dump truck. After a while, I was put into a tractor-trailer, a Flow-Boy. Flow Boys have a live floor, which functions like a conveyer belt, moving asphalt or dirt from the front of the trailer to the back and out the doors, sometimes on the ground at a construction site or into a machine that spreads out the asphalt for the rollers to roll it down. But that was a seasonal job, so I worked there during the season and then went to another job. One off-season, I went to a job where I hauled cars on a car hauler, which is a tractor-trailer designed to carry cars! At this job, I trained for about three weeks. The owner's son, the co-owner, drove with me the first week to teach me how to operate and use the truck. We would go to auto auctions and watch as dealers bid on the cars, and then we would drive them off the compound and into the parking lot, where we would begin loading the truck. I was told that we should have loaded the cars we were going to unload first on the back of the truck and the cars we were going to unload last on the front. While loading, he would show me the hydraulic levers and what they all did; there were some flaps on the end of the ramps that were in the up position. We put them in the place where they belong before driving a car on the ramp. The first car on the bottom of the truck was not that hard. We got them on, and then we set the pens on the truck so that when we put the cars on the top, we would not have to worry about the ramps coming down on the cars on the bottom ramp causing damage. The first car on the top of the truck had to be backed onto the truck, which was a little scary when I had to do it, but I had to learn! The most difficult part was not being able to use the mirrors. The side of the truck would take them right off! We had to open the door just enough to see the platform on the side of the car and then crawl out and onto the ramp to chain down the body of the car. You chain down the back of the car first, which was on the front of the truck; the back of the car hung over the top of the truck, then I chained down the back of the car. After loading, we had a measuring rod to make sure that the height was correct at thirteen feet and six inches. We took a load from Mannheim, Pennsylvania, to another auction location. This one was much bigger than the one in New York; it was so big that they had rides going from the parking lot to the auction house! It also was the first time I got a chance to see a Bentley! At first, I thought it was a Rolls Royce, but the grill was too low! But then I spotted the big 'B' surrounded by two wings! And I thought to myself, *that is what a Bentley looks like!* Well, well. When the auction was done, we loaded up the cars that the dealer bought and went to deliver them to their dealership. The next week, we drove different trucks. I had one, and the owner had one. He helped me load the truck that I was driving, and then we loaded the one he was to drive. I then delivered some of the cars locally and some to other little towns in the area. I also went to pick up some more cars and then went back to Mannheim to unload. The next week (week number three), I was on my own! I picked up about five vans and took them to Connecticut and Rhode Island; three went to Rhode Island, and the other two went to Connecticut. I had one load that was particularly unnerving! I loaded up in ADESA Auto Auction near Rochester, New York. After loading the truck, I noticed the space between the bottom of the car on top of the truck and the ramp of the truck was tight; you could hardly see any space there. I was confident that the car was bound well and tight! The road was a little bumpy, and I could see the car in the front was showing a little more space between the car and the top of the truck. It was as though the chains had loosened up some, so I kept an eye on it! A little farther down the road, there was more space up there! I began to wonder what was going on.

After some time, When I hit a bump, the car reacted slower than the truck; when the truck dropped on the downside of the bump, the car dropped after it, rather than with it, like an independent bounce! There was something wrong! I stopped at a service plaza on the highway to see what the problem might have been. When I looked at it, I saw that the car was higher than the way I put it on! I noticed other drivers looking in my direction and decided I needed to find out what was going on up there! I climbed the truck and examined the chain-up job I had done; clearly, something was wrong! I then found the problem. The front chains and the back chains were pulling in the same direction. The car was being pulled over the front of the truck! I undid the chains and redid them! That fixed the problem, and I was able to safely continue with the run. At one of my stops, about stop number two, a car on the top of the truck, just before the last one to be unloaded, had a dead battery! The place where I was to unload was closed, and it was late at night, with no one to contact! So, I had to figure out how to get that car off the truck! I looked over the hydraulic levers on the truck and calculated the effects of gravity, and then I raised the ramps in the front of the car and moved the movable parts of the ramps so that when I lowered the back of the ramps, the car would roll down to the next level of the trailer that was working. But then I noticed the car was getting too close to the side of the trailer on the left side! I stood back and tried to figure out what to do next. *How do I get a car that is not running to go back up a ramp?* Then it came to me. If I lower the front of the ramps, straighten the wheels, and raise the back of the ramps, the car will roll back up and line up with the ramps! After that, I was able to get back to my original plan of using the hydraulic levers and gravity to unload the car! I got the car off and moved it out of the way! I put the other car that was behind it back on the truck, checked all the pins to lock the ramps in place, and continued my run. One Christmas, I decided to get the young lady that I was going with at that time a remote starter for her car. I drove her car to work that day. At work, on the way to get a load of cars, I loaded her car on the trailer and took it to a car dealership and had them put one in her car, and I told them that I would pick it up when I returned. I returned two days later. I stopped, put her car back on the truck, and went back to the terminal. I unloaded her car and got ready to go home.

Chapter 15

Return to Construction

I was told when I started working at this job I would not have to sleep in the truck; instead, I would be put up in a hotel on the company's dime. We also had a fuel card. And after ninety days, I would get on their medical plan. After a while, I noticed that I was sleeping in the truck more often than in hotels; I had to start using cash for fuel, which they gave me at the start of the run! And at the end of the ninety days, I was told that I would not be getting medical insurance and that no one had it; they somehow lost it! I decided that I would have to find a company that has medical insurance. When I got home, I surprised my lady with the gift that I had got her. She was appreciative of the gift; no more going out in the cold to start up her car. I decided to return to RVA, driving construction vehicles, and they took me back! There were some fresh faces around now, and some of the old ones were still there too. I was put in a flow boy tractor-trailer, and I started hauling asphalt for a road contract they had going on at that time! Laying down hot asphalt all day long! I was even putting in some overtime; sometimes, I would work a double and then a half shift and take the next day off. I made friends with some of the guys there, and I even noticed a couple of young ladies working there as drivers now too! There were four of us that seemed to end up on the same job site a lot. One day as we were doing a highway job, I pulled up behind another one of our trucks; we were off-road on a job site, but he stopped right in front of me, so I made a move to go around him. That's when I found out that flow boy tractor-trailers turned a little different than regular tractor-trailers; they have fixed tandems, so they turned shorter than what I've been used to, and as I was going past his truck on my right, I suddenly started hearing metal and glass breaking. What I saw made me cringe! I was tearing up a BMW utility vehicle! Later, I learned that it belonged to the boss of that construction site! Well, he was not incredibly happy about that, but he and my company worked it out; I felt low the rest of the day. The guys at the job jazzed me for a long time over that! But as time went on, so did we. One of the guys there told me that he had a motorcycle that he was selling, I told him I did not have the money right now, but I did want to buy one, one day! He told me that since we were working together, I did not have to pay it all at once! That started to sound good to me, so I asked him how much he was selling it for. He said, for me, he would let it go for $500. Now it started to sound too good to pass up! So, one day after work, we went over to where he had the bike parked. It was a Red Ninja Kawasaki 1000 A.

Now the only riding I had ever done before that was in 1966 when one of my classmates from school let me ride while he sat on the back! But now, here I am, on my own! I was told that he could tell me how to ride, but he could not hold it up for me! I said *OK*! I got on the bike, and he told me about the gears, the clutch, and the brakes; he said that the gas was on the right handlebar! He asked, "Are you ready to ride?" I said, "Yes!" He told me to turn the key to the on position to see if it was in neutral; there was a green light showing, letting me know that it was out of gear! I then turned the key all the way and pushed the starter button; it had an electric starter, and when it started, I let it run for a bit. Then, I was ready to ride! Its gear pattern was one down and five up! Easy enough, I thought, so I put it in gear by tapping down the gear lever and started letting it out on the clutch. It was on the left handlebar. And the bike started rolling! Keeping it upright was not hard; it straightened up on its own! I pressed in the clutch, and with the top of my left foot, I tapped the gear shifter up and released the clutch. I was doing well for riding for the first time on my own! I got up to third gear, and everything was going great, but now, I was coming to a T in the road! I stopped at the end of the road to make sure the way was clear, and then the guy I was buying the bike from made a left-hand turn. As I followed, I realized that the bike was not turning; it was still going straight! There were no vehicles coming, but I was headed right at a building on the other side of the street! I kept trying to turn the bike, but it would not turn! The curb was getting closer and closer, so I pressed the lever on the left side of the handlebars, and the bike seemed to speed up! *That lever was not the brakes! That was the clutch! I took the bike out of gear!* I got nervous and tried to stop the bike by putting my feet on the ground and pulling back to stop it, but that only caused my thigh joints to hurt! The bike weighed 530 pounds, and it was moving! For some reason, I could not remember that the front brake was on the right side, and the back brake was by my right foot! The hand brake and the foot brake, I hit the curb just as I figured it out! I hit the curb, and the bike bounced and wiggled! But I recovered, got straight, and acted like nothing was wrong. I started riding again. I quickly caught up with Dion; it was him that I was buying the bike from. We rode around town without any more mishaps. After a while, I parked the bike in my mom's backyard. There were times when I would go out by myself and ride around. Once, when I was out riding, I stopped by a friend's house to show off my bike. I stopped on the sidewalk in front of his house, got off my bike, and started walking toward him, but I noticed that my bike was falling over. I had forgotten to put the kickstand down! My friend and another guy who was on his bike in the driveway said, "Your bike is falling! Watch out!" But before it could hit the ground, I got a grip on it and struggled with it. I realized just how heavy 520 pounds could get when it is leaning over like that. But I did get it up before it hit the ground. I felt so stupid for forgetting to put my kickstand down before turning my bike loose! Another time, when I was riding alone again, I pulled into a parking lot that was empty just to chill for a while. I got close to the curb of the parking lot and almost hit it; I came close to falling off the bike, trying to stop it. Since I was headed home, I decided to go and park it. The next day or two, I rode it to work. One day I was told that they had all their drivers reported for work that day, and they would not need me. I thought to myself, *I am an extra*. I was under the impression that I was a regular! I got upset and decided to find another job somewhere. Not long after that, I found another job. I heard of a company that was starting a new branch; it would be hauling trash. They had a different type of tractor-trailer hookup; the trailer was called a walking floor. They had an open top and a live floor. I was one of the first five drivers to be employed by this company for that position. We would go into places like Brooklyn, New York, and Vermont to load trash from a transfer station and unload it at a landfill in upstate New York. We would start on a Sunday night to get to Brooklyn ahead of the traffic, but the ride over would be an adventure within itself! I liked driving at night better than in the daytime, so that was no problem for me! The first trip out was interesting. After pre-tripping the unit, I was instructed on how the walking floor worked, how to connect the wet lines, the hoses that the hydraulic fluid would flow to operate the floor, and the operation of the doors. The back door had an inner door that was to remain open as we were driving empty. To cut down on the wind drag, we would open it and latch it to the inside of the trailer. When we were ready to be loaded, we would unlatch it, close it, and fasten it to the surrounding door. We needed to have the truck out of gear, with the brakes on, then engage the lever to operate the floor! And we had a long removable handle to roll or unroll a tarp to cover or uncover the load. We also received directions to our pickup sites, and we were on our way. We had to go into Brooklyn, New York, to get a load of garbage! We left and took I-390 South, then Route 15, south and seventeen, east until 15 and 17 split up! We then took seventeen through Binghamton, New York, and rode through some small towns until we reached I-84. Then we took that east and went onto I-87 South. It was a tollway with traffic going north and south; 87 took us into I-287 and across the Tappan Zee bridge. That went over the Hudson River and headed towards White Plains, New York. After that, we stayed on I-287 and I-87. There were some amazing things to see in New York! I drove right by the Yankee Stadium, the George Washington Bridge, and JFK Airport. I saw Manhattan on my right and signs for Long Island. I went across the Tri-borough Bridge and into Brooklyn, where I exited for Varick Avenue. I had to go to 215 Varick avenue, where the transfer station was, to get my load information. I had to park on a nearby street and walk into the shipping office.

I was told to pull into the gates and onto the scale for my weight and then park and wait to be called. When I was called, I was told to go into the building to be loaded and then pull back up on the scale; if my weight was off, I would have to go back into the building to have it adjusted and then back on the scale, and so on until it was correct! After that, I had tarped the trailer for travel and did my logs; you always must do your logs! And then headed out. I had to stop in Binghamton because I ran out of hours on my logs, and I was too early for my appointment to unload. There were also no places to park and wait. I would park at a TA truck stop and get something to eat and some sleep. The next morning, I headed out to the landfill; we had different ones to go to. This time, we were going to Seneca Meadows. When we arrived, the first thing we did was line up to get on the scale, then pull up and out of the way to un-tarp the trailer. We had to put our radios on channel three to hear the loader operators for unloading instructions. When I was called, I went up the hill; it seemed like a long way up, but finally, I reached the spot where I was told to back up to an area where another truck had just finished unloading! I backed up, opened my door, went to the front of the trailer, in between the tractor and the trailer to connect the hydraulic lines, then to the tractor to raise the RPMs, and finally back to the trailer to walk the load off! Back in the truck, I let the trailer do its job! After unloading, I was told to go over to a spot that was set aside to sweep out the trailer, close the door, unhook hydraulic lines, and head on down the hill. I did four of those a week! Not too bad on the pay. There were times when we were sent to other places to pick up loads. We went to a place in Brooklyn called Red Hook to pick up loads going to Chaffee, New York! We also sometimes would go to Vermont to get loaded with demolition and take it to the incinerator in Buffalo. I went to a lot of places to pick up trash. One day, I got word that one of the other drivers, another of the five who started out with this company when it first started, had an accident. I always called him Sly because his name was Sylvester. When I asked if he was okay, I was told he was dead! That came as such a shock! We had done a lot of runs together and were becoming friends. And now I hear that he is dead! He was just talking about closing on a house, and he like I was supposed to be off that day! I was told that he was on the way back from New York with a load that he was going to unload the following Monday when, for some reason, he lost control of his truck, turned over on the driver's side, and slid into a concrete guard rail and was pinned down so that he could not breathe, and suffocated! I thought that had to be a bad way to go! I mean, dying in any way would be bad, but being pinned so that you could not get any air! It brought tears to my eyes; I did not even want to drive anymore! And I did not know for about three weeks or so. The boss, Nick, kept telling me that it could have happened to anyone! But I was thinking I should stop driving trucks and find something else to do! But Nick said that if I wanted to, I could drive dump trucks and haul salt, so that is what I did for a little while. In the dump truck, I would go to the salt mine in Mount Morris, New York, and get loaded with salt. The truck had a pup-trailer on the back, and I had to load both! One of the other drivers guided me on what to do. We went into the office and talked to the office workers about the load, and they told me what I was to do. I got back in the truck and followed the other driver around to the loading area. When my turn came, I pulled under the hoppers and positioned myself for the first drop; my instructions were to get three drops in the truck and two in the trailer and then get on the scale to check my weight. After that, I used a tarp to cover both the truck and the trailer. We took the salt-to-salt barns in some of the little towns in and around Rochester. Dumping the truck was interesting too! I backed the truck into a shed and dumped the trailer first and then pulled up so that I could angle the trailer out of the way of the truck, then dumped the truck! That was a first for me. When I pulled forward, the pup ran over the salt while getting back in line with the truck. Finally, after a while, the guy that I worked for talked me into going back to walking floors, and I started going back to Brooklyn and the landfills and making the big bucks again. Once while returning from Brooklyn with a load of trash, I, along with two other drivers, stopped at a little hole-in-the-wall truck stop. There was a young lady working at the fuel station that caught our attention. Her body was so attractive that we all had trouble being tactful in our behavior. I became quite attracted to her. I became an animal. I just wanted to get next to her, if only for a little while, even just once! But I did not! I was not alone in those thoughts, but there was one problem. Her face was not as nice looking like her body. If I were to get with her, I would not have wanted anyone to know, and again, I was not the only person with that opinion either. It was just a sexual attraction, I did not think that it would be right to treat her in that matter, so neither of us took it any further. I have seen the time when that would not have stopped me. I mean that there were times when every woman or every woman that was willing was excepted, But I have changed. I worked for one company that had a different pay scale than any other company that I had ever worked with before! I was paid a percentage of what the load paid. One such company was Landstar Inway. I filled out an application, and it was accepted; I was sent to Pittsburgh, Pennsylvania, for orientation.

Chapter 16

Percentage

I drove my personal vehicle to the orientation, and the company paid for a hotel as well as reimbursement for the use of my personal vehicle to get there and back, as well as for food during the orientation period. After I returned home, I started getting calls from fleet owners offering me job opportunities. Landstar did not have trucks, but they had the contacts, and they had to accept the drivers before a fleet owner could put you to work. I was called one day by a fleet owner in Pennsylvania. I inquired about the pay and my duties, and all his answers sounded good! He said that I would be driving a Western Star tractor with a sleeper. He had me catch a bus to his location, then put me in a hotel for the night. When I got off the bus, the fleet owner met me, we drove to the hotel and said that we would get together the following day, and then he would give me the low down on the job and get the truck. As I got a look at the hotel, I wondered, *was this the best he could do?* The hotel looked like, at some time in the past, it was a barn or something! Then I thought he was trying to save money, or this was the closest one to us. The next morning, he came by to pick me up, and we went to the truck, which was a let-down too! It was a Western Star, but an old Western Star! But I was still willing to give it a shot. Well, the next thing was, the truck would not start! We had to jump-start it. When we got it running, I was told that I would be picking up the load in my hometown the next morning at the Kodak building on Lexington Avenue. So, I drove the truck home and parked in front of my mother's house. It was cold that night, so I packed some extra clothes. The next morning, I loaded my stuff into the truck, and when I turned the key, the truck did not start. I called the owner to let him know so he would have time to let the shipper know and get someone there to fix it. I went into the house and waited to get the truck fixed. When the guy got the truck running, I let it warm up and then headed out to the shipper. When about two blocks away from my house, the truck stopped again, and I could not get it started! To me, that was the final limit! I called and told the owner to let him know that the truck was down again! Now, I am thinking, *what if this happens and I am out in some secluded area, in the cold? No, I cannot do this!* I called the owner back and told him that was not going to work, and he would have to send someone to get his truck because I was not going to work for him! I then packed my stuff up and went back home. I was extremely disappointed with that experience and wondered if I should have just gone back to one of the companies I had worked with before. But not long after that, I got a call from another fleet owner with Landstar. This one was in Maryland. I asked him some questions about the offer, like what kind of truck and what kind of pay, and all the answers returned favorably, so I accepted the job. I was sent a ticket to Baltimore on a train; It had been a while since I was on a train. It gave me a feeling of déjà vu. I think, if I remember correctly, my last trip on a train was when I was about six or seven years old! That was the first time I left my mother to go and live with my grandma in Florida! I do not remember much about that time in my life! But I remember my cousin Aretha took me down with her after one of her visits with my mother. I remember setting on the train and looking out of the window. I was looking at my mom standing there crying, and I remember thinking she might want to change her mind and take me off the train, and it made me cry too! I was ready to travel, and she wanted to stop me. I was her oldest child, the firstborn of her and my father. My father died when I was about three or four years old, and now here I am, on a train about to leave her too! But all I could see was that I was going on a trip somewhere, and the excitement had taken over my will, and I was ready to go. I do not remember the time I had with my cousin! All I remember was the truck that my cousin put me in when I left her house was a pulpwood truck, and it took me right to the front yard of my grandma's house. My memory of the years before my first year of school is cloudy and spotty. Now here I am, on a train again, going to another state. This time, for a job. I wondered if I was making the right move. Is this going to be another bummer? This was the same company, just a different fleet owner. I decided to go to the restaurant part of the train, and I went to find something to eat. This was different also! While I was in transit, I was able to walk from one car to the next to a place to get something to eat. In the meal car, I found a sandwich and got something to drink. I sat down and ate as I looked out of the window. There was not much to look at. I could not see anything because it was nighttime! After finishing, I went back to my seat. When I got to Baltimore, I met up with the fleet owner, and he drove me over to Hagerstown, Maryland, where he lived. In his office, he gave me the rundown on the job. I was still wondering, *what did the truck look like?* After that last one, I was jaded. I was thinking, *I hope this one is at least drivable!* When we got to the truck, I was pleasantly surprised! It was a Peter Built 379, 62-inch walk-in sleeper with an extended hood and a thirteen-speed transmission, all black! *A show truck! Now that's what I'm talking about! Now that is a truck!* He had it parked at a truck stop in Hagerstown. I received my orders, pre-tripped the truck, and started out on my way. My first load had to go to Houston, Texas. Driving this truck was a little different yet fun; with a thirteen-speed transmission, it had a dog leg and a splitter! It was in the shape of an eight-speed; you get your first four gears out, pull up the dog leg, split the last eight, and have low gear.

Sometimes when I was empty, I would shift it like an eight-speed. I would get the last gear with the splitter. I remember one time I was just cruising down the road when some trucks started to catch up with me. They were going fast and talking on their citizen band radios; they started passing me up convoy style! As they were pulling away, I decided to see what this truck could do! I hit the splitter and dropped a gear, got on the fuel pedal, and started to wind it out, and then I picked up another gear. Before they got too far up the road, I was starting to match their speed, and then I was gaining on them. I was starting to pass them up, one at a time, then I noticed that I was now pulling away from them! I felt good. I was the big dog for a change! My truck was going faster than all of them! I was satisfied; I realized I had a big truck, and it could run! So, I slowed back down to an acceptable rate of speed and just relaxed and enjoyed the ride. On the way to Houston, I remembered a truck stop on the other side of New Orleans on I-10. There was a truck stop called Tigers, and I decided that I would stop for a break when I got there. I got a chance to see a large tiger; he looked as though he did not want to be bothered. He remained laying down with his head facing away from view and his back turned towards the open side of the cage! So, I went into the restaurant to get a bite. I had eaten so much; I had gumbo, fish, red beans and rice, hush puppies, and crayfish etouffee. I was so full that I had to go to the truck and get some sleep. I could not sleep long because I had to get on down the highway. After I reached my destination, I got unloaded and then headed to my next stop. At this stop, I picked up some food-grade products and headed to New Jersey. Riding on my way to my next stop, I was somewhere in Virginia when I heard a large bang. I knew right away what it was; I had a flat! Yep, I had a flat tire on the trailer, the last tire on the right outside. I called the owner to inform him of my situation. He made a call, then got back to me to say that help was on the way. He also told me to keep the tire after it was replaced and to put it in the trailer so I could return it to him. After the flat was fixed, I put the other tire in the back, and I was on my way again. Finally, I reached my drop-off point. I went and reported into the dock area, and I was told to back up to the dock. After I opened the trailer doors, the loader saw the tire! At once, he refused the load. He said that he could not take it because I had a tire inside the trailer with food-grade stuff. He turned it down cold! I had the fleet owner call him. When the fleet owner called me back, he said that it was his fault for telling me to put the tire in the trailer with food-grade products, then he said that we would have to return it. He also said that he would pay me because it was his fault. So, I took the load back to Houston. After a little wait, I received my orders for another load. It was close by, a load of plants going over by Buffalo, New York. When I got to where I was to load, there was no dock; there was a dirt ramp that I had to back up to. They got me loaded, and I was on my way north. Sometimes getting paid by the percentage is better than getting paid by the mile, but there are times when the mile is better. For example, the load of plants I brought from Houston to Buffalo paid less than another load I had that came from Connecticut and went to Erie, Pennsylvania, and it only had four pallets, whereas the load from Houston to Buffalo had eighteen pallets. As by mile, the load from Houston and went to Buffalo would have paid more, but I like the percentage better. There was one trip that I was on where I was on the way to California. I was going through Indiana when I came upon a backup on I-70 Westbound; there was an extensive line of traffic before me, and nobody was going anywhere. I heard on the CB about a way around it. About that time, I saw some other trucks getting off at the next exit, and I started following them. We got off and started going on a local highway. I do not know how many other trucks were ahead of me, but I was able to see three plus myself! There was a Martin refrigerator truck just ahead of me, and it was going so slow that the other two trucks were pulling away from us! I started to worry about if the truck in front of me was not taking the bypass but going to a place over there for some other purposes. By then, I saw the two other drivers ahead of us making a right turn and about to go out of my site! Then the lane opened into two lanes, so I downshifted and started passing the Martin truck. I kept looking in my right mirror and back in front of me until I cleared him. As I was passing him, I asked him why he was going so slow. He responded that he saw a police officer and that he did not want to get a ticket for speeding! I said, "I heard that!" At that time, I noticed that the lanes started to turn back to one lane again, And I was still passing his truck! So, I put my foot down and completed the pass. As I moved back in line, I saw a lady on the sidewalk looking at me, and at the same time, I saw a sign that said the speed limit was 35 mph! I was going about 60 mph, and I looked in my left mirror, and to my shock, there was a police officer following me with his red lights flashing! Yeah, I was in trouble! I was being pulled over! So, I found a safe place on the side of the road and stopped. When the officer got to me, he said, "Let me see your license, logbook and registration, insurance, and your load information!" I handed him my license, and as he received it, he said, "You know you won't be getting this back, right?" I told him that I was on my way to California, and he said that I would have to ride with the ticket! I did not question it. I took the ticket and completed the run. After I finished the run and got the backhaul that went to Euclid, Ohio, I called my dispatch for my next load. I was told that he was still working on it. After a while, he told me that he could not find anything. He then said that I should come back to Hagerstown, Maryland, empty. I felt funny about that, from Euclid, Ohio, to Hagerstown, Maryland, empty? Something is wrong with this picture! I got to Hagerstown and went to the Pilot Truck Stop, where we normally parked the truck. It was late, so I crawled back into the bed and went to sleep. The next morning, my employer showed up, and I mentioned my curiosity about driving all that way empty. He just looked down at the ground, and then he said that Landstar told him that I could not work for them anymore! That was an awkward situation, I thought! I am being fired! Wow, I do not want to take my stuff back home on a train! He said I could leave my stuff in his office and return to get it in my car, which I did. And after that, I was jobless again. My next job was one that I had been working for before: *Metalico*! Working local means, I would be home every night to sleep in my own bed. I can get comfortable with that. I had been with this company before; this time, there were some changes; there were some new drivers along with the ones that were here when I left. The people in the office had changed a little too! At orientation, I was introduced to the team, and I filled out some more paperwork. Since I was there before, I did not need to be trained again, so I just started working. I was pulling dump trailers, and sometimes, I would drive a Roll-off truck. I even asked if they would let me train on the shear crane if things were slow for the dump trailers and roll-off trucks. When I got the chance to get in one, I was trained step-by-step on what to do, starting with a pre-trip inspection of the machine and checking the oil, hydraulic fluid, and fuel level. And then, inside the machine to check the gauges and controls, I was pleased to see that it had a radio, tinted glass, heater, and air conditioning!

Chapter 17

Metalico

After we pre-tripped the crane, I was shown how to test the hydraulics by operating the arm, jaw, and swivels, rotating the crane in a circle to the right and then back to the left, raising and lowering the arm, and swiveling it clockwise and counterclockwise. I then sat in the seat and put on the seatbelt. I got comfortable and started to cut steel; some were beams, and some were just long pieces of metal too large to put in a trailer or a roll-off box. My job was to cut it so that it would be the right size to load. It took me a little time to get the hang of it, but then I was doing it. I was cutting steel and having fun doing it! I was listening to some nice music on the radio, and I had the air conditioning on because it was warm that day. I felt like I was in a Tonka toy, working the levers and the pedals. I was told that whenever I would go in reverse, I should always turn the vehicle in the direction I wanted to go so that I could see better. Even with the rear-view mirrors, the crane is so large that it would be difficult to see behind me.

There were a couple of times that I would let the jaws of the crane down too far, and it would hit the ground and shake me up a bit. But I would keep cutting steel.

After a while, someone came to let me know that it was break time. I was shocked. *Break time? Break from what?* I felt like I was already on break! This was easy compared to doing roll-off work! But I took my break with everyone else. I was asked, "How did you like running a crane?" I said, "It was cool. I will get the hang of it before long." After the break, I went back to the crane and got back to the job at hand. I did that for two days, and I felt as though I was doing all right, but at the end of the day, I was told that I would have to return to my old position. They told me that I was not doing the job as well as they needed! I was going too slow! So, now it was back to the roll-off and tractors. One run I had in a roll-off, I was to take an empty roll-off box to a place that I had never been to before! It was out in the woods! When I got there, I saw that it was on a farm, way back in the back of a house, in a field, and it was raining that day. I was told where to drop off the empty, and they told me about the other one that I was to pick up. I got out of the truck and unstrapped the box, got back in the truck, raised the boom on the truck, and unloaded the empty. I then lowered the boom and got into position for the loaded one. After raising the boom and backing up to the box, I got out and hooked the cable to the box, got back into the truck, and started pulling the box onto the truck. The box was heavy, and I had some trouble getting it on the truck. After I got the box on the truck, I got out and strapped it to the truck. When I started to leave, the truck would not go! It was stuck in the mud! I had tried everything to get it going, but nothing worked! So, I got out of the truck and looked at what I could do to free myself! I produced an idea! I took the straps off the box, got back in the truck, and raised the box up some. I then released the cable a little at a time until the box was touching the ground. I released the brakes and slowly loosened the cable. The weight of the box was enough to start moving the truck. And then, I put the brakes on the truck and pulled the box back into the truck. I repeated that until the truck was in a solid spot, and then I loaded the box back into the truck and strapped it down. The guy that I was getting the load from seemed to be impressed with how I got the truck out and on the road. That is a case of the levers and hydraulics helping me out again. I used levers and hydraulics a lot with this job! I had a tractor with a roll-off trailer and loading and unloading required the use of levers and hydraulics! With a tractor, you had to make sure the wheels were straight, or you would have a big problem on your hands. The trailer had a switch that worked like a brake, so if you were to unload a box, you could slowly walk the truck away from the box! When you get to where you want to unload the box, you unstrap it from the trailer, use the switch on the trailer to lock the brakes, take the brakes off the truck, raise the power take off, and make sure the truck wheels are straight! And then go back to the trailer and start raising the boom. When you have the boom up enough, start releasing the cable. As the box touches the ground, release the brakes to let the box push the truck. If it starts rolling too fast, apply the brakes to stop it. I would repeat this until I got the box off! Then I would unhook the cable and lower the boom. Most of the time, I would have to pick up a loaded one too! So, I would position myself in front of the full box, raise the boom so that it is low enough for the rollers on the box to set in place, put the hook on the box, set the brakes on the trailer, release the brakes on the truck, making sure that the wheels are straight as well on the tractor! Tighten the cable pulling the box, release the trailer brakes, and let the box pull the truck under it, lowering the boom as needed until the box is on the trailer, strap the box to the trailer, put the truck brakes on, and release the trailer brakes. Most times, I would have to tarp the box so that nothing could fly out on the highway as I returned to the scrapyard.

Chapter 18

There was one time when I was pulling a walking floor trailer loaded with metal shavings headed for Pittsburgh, Pennsylvania. I was passing through Buffalo, and at the other side of the tollbooth, a Trooper stopped me. He said that my trailer was littering the highway with material and leaking some stuff all over the highway. He asked to see my papers and told me that I was not to haul the truck, and he found a problem with my license. He said that my license had been dropped down to a class D and that I was not to drive a tractor-trailer until the problem was fixed! My company had to pick me up and send someone to take the truck to one of their partner's locations to deliver it. The next day, I called the Department of Motor Vehicles to find out the problem and was told that my physical card was out of date! I let them know that I just had it done! But I was told that no one filed it with them. That was the second time that had happened to me with this company. So, I went down and got it straight with them. Another time when I was told to take a walking floor out of a loading bay to have the aluminum shavings in the trailer adjusted, I backed up the tractor and hooked it up to the trailer, then hooked up the airlines and the electric line before raising the landing gear. I put the truck in gear and put on the trailer brake; then, I tried to pull forward to check the hookup, and everything went well. I then started pulling out of the bay. As I started to make a right turn, the trailer came loose. I stopped quickly, so the trailer landed on the truck's tires. I almost dropped the trailer! I put the brakes on and took the truck out of gear. I went back to see what was going on and what I could do to fix it! I started letting down the landing gear; I winded and winded until I was too tired to turn anymore, then someone else winded for a while. It took three of us to raise the trailer high enough to back the truck back under it.

Chapter 19

Another time when I was on the way back from Sidney, New York, I was a little way out from Binghamton when I heard a loud pop. I did not see any tire from where I was setting that would have made the noise, but the rig was not running right. I then decided to pull over to see what could be happening. As I started to pull over to the right side of the highway, the front of the truck felt like it was going to slide, so I took it easy, slowly moving to the right shoulder of the highway Just then, I saw a tire come rolling past me on my left. It passed me, just missed a passing car, and ended up in the median between the north and south bound lanes! I made it to the right shoulder and parked. I got out and walked around the truck from the driver's door and down the left side. All the tires were there. I checked the tractor tires, then the trailer tires on the left side moving around to the right side, and on to the truck tires on the right. As I made my way back to the driver's side to get in the truck, I spotted the problem! The tire had come off the rim of the front of the truck, on the driver's side! I made it to the shoulder of the highway on the rim, which is why the truck slid the way it did! I could've jack-knifed the rig. I called it in, and after a while, help came. He asked me if I wanted to use the rim that was on the truck. Since the tire did not blow, and we did not know what happened, I thought he should replace the rim also. This was a frighting experience, but I made it home unharmed. One day while I was at home, my wife at that time decided that she would like to move to Atlanta, Georgia. She said that her only daughter who lived there was about to go to France, a part of her studies for college, and she did not want to lose her apartment. After thinking about it for a few days, I told her if I could find a job down there that, I would not mind going to live there. My son was grown now, and there was nothing to hold me up here. So, I put in some applications, and after a while, I started getting responses, and I found one that I knew a little about.

Chapter 20

Relocating.

The recruiter said that all my paperwork that they had for now looked great, and that by the time I get down there, they should have the rest, and that I could come on down to start orientation. So, we sold some of the things we were not going to take with us that we did not really need, and we put the things we wanted but did not have room for in storage. And we took off for Atlanta. On the way, we stopped by my wife's brother's house in Pittsburg, Pennsylvania. We spent the night there, and the next day, we rode around; she showed me the neighborhood, and we went by her old school. Then back at her brother's house, we had something to eat and got some sleep. After we got up, we had breakfast, and we were on our way again. We stopped at a park that was at the beginning of a long free-hanging bridge and took a walk along the bridge trail to get a look. As a truck driver, I had crossed that bridge many times and wondered about it. There was a wooden walkway along the side of the gorge that went under the bridge; we walked about part way and looked at the river under it. Then, we headed back up to the car, a 2003 jeep grand Cherokee Laredo, and were on our way again. When we got to where the orientation was to be held, we were furnished with a hotel in the town that the job was in, Tunnel Hill, Georgia. We went out to get something to eat, and I found a restaurant that had an all-you-can-eat seafood buffet. I loaded up on crab legs, frog legs, and raw oysters and then went to bed. At orientation, we did paperwork and test drove the trucks while my wife was at the hotel. The recruiter told me at the end of the orientation that they could not hire me because they could not get enough proof of my driving record, and two jobs on my application could not be verified. Here I was, about 950 miles away from home, with no job, and the only money I had was my last paycheck, and I was thinking to myself, *what am I going to do now? I am down here with no money, a wife, and no job!* When we got to my wife's daughter's apartment in Atlanta, we found that it was a gated community, and we had to call her to get in. She gave us the code to the gate, and once inside the gate, we had to drive all the way to the back. From her front door, you could see the gate in one straight shot. We unloaded the car and went upstairs to the apartment. After we got settled in, I got on my computer to look over the area to see what was around because I had to find a job asap! That next Monday, I started making phone calls. One place I called was J.B. Hunt, and the recruiter asked some questions about my experience, and then he asked me why did I leave U.S. Express? I told him that I had never worked for them and that I only went there for orientation, but they could not hire me because they were unable to prove my work history.

Then he told me that if they could not get enough work history that he would have the same problem. So, I did not get the job there. I drove over to another company called SWIFT, filled out an app, and had an interview, and I was turned down there too! Things were starting to get disparate. I was now out of money and still had no job. I then decided to return to one of my previous jobs down there, but there was a chance they would not hire me again because I had quit twice. But they hired me again, and they let me bring my wife with me on my runs. This was working great; I got a chance to take my wife to my hometown in Florida. On the way to my hometown, we went by one of the little towns where I would party in my younger days. It was a small place, too, Folkston, Georgia. When we got to my hometown Hilliard, Florida, I drove past where my grandmother's house used to be, and then as we started to make the turn to go past my uncle's house, I found it difficult to make. It was too tight, and I struggled for a while trying to make that turn. I did not want to take down someone's mailbox or damage the truck. I was not supposed to be there anyway; how would I explain this to my company? I got out and looked around for a solution, and I noticed that the tandem wheels could be moved forward to make the pivot point shorter, so I had my wife pull the pin on the trailer tandems so that I could back the trailer up, which moved the tandems forward, and then we locked the pin in place and drove out of Hilliard. After a while, things started going wrong. The company would send me to pick up Avon products; I would go from Dalton, Georgia, to Suwanee, Georgia. And a lot of times, the load would not be ready for hours. Most of the time, your logbook would run out before you would get to your destination, but they would say that the load is hot, meaning that the load had to be there on time. I told them that I did not have enough log time to make that trip. After that, they would send me places and not have a load to come back for a long time. My checks started getting smaller and smaller until I had to start getting advances on my pay to survive. Then one day, the repo-man came to the terminal and repossessed my Jeep. After that, we used the truck for transportation to get from work to home and everywhere else. You know, when you are in a truck all the time with someone, there is a lot that you will learn about each other, sometimes more than you want to know! We were together at work, at home, and everywhere else. There were times when we got on each other's nerves, but overall, we made it from day to day. My wife was always with me whenever the truck moved, and if we stopped at a truck stop, I would make sure she was never left alone! But when we would go into a truck stop to take a shower, we would go into different rooms. I would worry about her the whole time I was showering. After showering, we would go to a restaurant and have a meal.

We would talk over the day's events and then head back to the truck to get some sleep so that we could start the next day's adventure. We would sometimes not even go to the apartment; instead, we would go to a truck stop with a park-n-view hook-up, which is where you can connect to cable and watch TV in the truck. Because of the lack of funds, we would not have gas and electricity at home. We were out there getting advances on my pay to survive, and having to pay it back, and having less and less to live on until we were living off advances! And to make matters worse, the company I was working for decided that us staying in the truck while we were so close to home was against company rules, and they started charging us for the time that we spent at the truck stops with the truck! All this in just three months! So, after that, it was time to let go, and I was job hunting again. I was walking all over Atlanta looking for a job; I put in applications to so many places and several types of jobs. I went to trucking companies. I also went to the airport to try to get a job with the T.S.A. and even a shoe store in the airport to sell shoes. I went to a bus company and a security guard job. I went to two junk yards, a steel company. Finally, it was down to going to food barns to get food and government agencies to get money for rent and power; we were almost homeless at that point. My wife got a job at the airport until she got fed up going all the way to the airport with public transportation at night, and I did not feel like it was safe for her to be out at night away from me like that somewhere in Atlanta. Next, she got a job at a coffee shop across the street from the apartment. She had to leave that job because they were pushing her too hard and said that she was not moving fast enough. Meanwhile, I was back on the phone trying to do the truck driver thing again, and then one day, I called J.B. Hunt again, and since I had that time with my last company, I had enough experience to qualify for an interview with them. It started out like it always does; the hotel, the orientation, the paperwork, the physical, and then you get a truck. The hotel had nothing special to talk about; two of us to a room, and a van would come and pick us up for orientation and then drop us back off at night. At orientation, we had our physical and drug tests and the rest of the paperwork for the job. On the drug test, they had to get a hair sample; the hair sample came from my chest because they did not want to mess up my beard, and I shaved my head. We had to do stress tests like walking in place for a few minutes and climbing. I was told some of our runs were stressful, and they did not want us to have a heart attack or something. We would go out and do a driving test which took us by Evander Holyfield's House. I was driving as we passed it, so I did not get a good look. After a while, we were ready to start out on our own. I got my first load at some well-known places, one being the Duracell Battery company. The money was all right, but not what I expected for being over the road and sleeping in a truck for a lot of the time! I was thinking to myself that there must be a better way! And then, one day, a message came over the onboard computer about a program called 90 days (about 3 months) walk away lease. I was noticing the money that was being made from some of these loads I picked up was not bad! I knew if I were making it like that, I could pay for a truck without a problem! So, when I got back in from that run, I inquired about the program. I asked if I would be making enough money to pay for the truck. I should have asked if I were making enough to pay off the truck and take care of my business away from the job too! But I did not! I got into the program and went to work. I saw one invoice that was for $3,000.00. And that was just one load on that run! I was thinking that I would be getting a good piece of that on my pay. WRONG! I got about $500.00 that week! When I got my settlement, I saw that I was paying for the lease for the truck, maintenance and pre-maintenance, legal papers, plates, accountants, and uses of the dispatch equipment. Although I got a discount on the fuel, it was not that much. I had no money at the end of the week to send home for my own bills! I kept telling myself that it would get better after a while; I just needed to keep running. I tried to find runs on my own, but every time I found something, I was told that the loads I found did not pay enough. I began to feel like I should have just cut my losses and ended the lease, returning to being a company driver so that I could at least have some money. I met another driver who said that the lease thing was a ploy! He said that they use that same truck, and every three months, they would put someone else in it with the same game so that someone else would always be paying off that same truck! I do not have to tell you... I felt like a real sucker! I got caught up in a game! I was being used! I was just trying to do right, and I was not out trying to get something for nothing. I was not out there mugging people or taking advantage of somebody. I was working, trying to pay my bills, and take care of my wife. I was just trying to make a living.   I decided to call in and give my notice because when I signed up for that job, I was told that I would have to let them know 30 days before the lease's 90 days were up, and I was 60 days in and had not been home in a while. When I contacted them to let them know my plans about ending the lease, I was told that my next time off was four weeks away! *WHAT? I have been out for two months without going home! I am on blood pressure meds, and my prescription has run out!* I was asked, "How long would you need?" I told them that I did not know because the doctor would have to check me out. Finally, they agreed and let me go home. On the way home, I called my wife and told her to get a ride and meet me at the MARTA station at the Kensington stop. When I got there, she was there in a jeepney. I took my stuff out of the truck and told her that I would be back in a while. She said OK. When I got the truck back to the terminal, I turned the truck in, then I walked to the MARTA bus stop and took it to the airport where I caught the Marta train there and road to

Five Points to the Atlanta MARTA station in the heart of Atlanta! This is where you can catch a train going in all directions of Atlanta. Downstairs is a tourist attraction called Underground Atlanta. I caught the train for Avondale Station and stayed within walking distance to the train station. After a couple of days at home, I got a call from the company asking me when I was coming back. In which I said that I would not be! They said that I would have to pay for the truck! And I let them know that I had returned the truck before my 90 days were up and that I did not want the truck. I was told that the lenders would come after me for the money, and I said that they would have to do what they had to do. And just like that, I was out of work again. After about a week or so, I found another job. It was a company owned by a young lady, a nice-looking young lady. I must say, she was left the company by her father after he passed away.

Chapter 21

She had two trucks. The trucks were on the old side but not too bad overall. Another driver was starting on the same day as I was. The trucks were behind the two houses, in the backyard, and they were both road trucks, so when we had to go to sleep, they had beds in the back. It was like starting all over again, with a new company and a new job! The significant difference was I had to pay more attention to the paperwork, fuel receipts, and any other bills I'd paid for. I found that out when I came back after a two-week turn. I was unable to account for some of the money I spent on the run, so it came out of my pay! Meanwhile, my wife at that time was complaining about me being gone for so long; she acted as if I were messing with my boss. No matter what I said, I could not convince her that I was not. It seemed like every week; I had the same challenge of trying to let her know that I was working. After a while, my employer got a contract with FedEx, and we had to go in for orientation which lasted for about three days. We would have to stay in a hotel for that time, but before that, we had to get the trucks qualified, worked on, and inspected. The whole time, my wife kept complaining that I was spending too much time with my boss and saying things like, "Why would you have to be the one to take the truck to be prepared? It was not your truck!" I kept telling her that the company was a small one, and since I would be driving the truck, I had to drive it to be worked on so that it would be ready for the job. At the orientation, we were not the only company there; we met with other truck owners and the drivers that they had with them, and then the paperwork and the rules according to FedEx. One of the truck owners was a cute little lady from Fontana, California, and another owner from Las Vegas, Nevada, was trying to impress the young lady from Fontana, which struck me funny. After she told him she had somebody, he backed off. Then we talked about it and had a laugh. At the end of the orientation, we exchanged contact information, and he said that he paid his drivers a thousand dollars a week. I thought to myself that was more than the young lady was paying, and I would not have to worry about my wife thinking that I was trying to date my boss. After working about two to three weeks on this new arrangement, I did not see any improvement in the pay, and there was a lot of sitting time between runs. On one run, I sat so long that my wife started to complain. She said that I was gone all the time, and the money was not showing that I was working, and bills were due. I told her I could not help because I was not getting the runs. The conversation quickly devolved into an argument, to the point where she stated that she was considering divorce. That was hard to hear. I was out there on the road trying to make a living for us, and she acted like I was on vacation or something. I kept telling the young lady I was driving for that I needed to get home. I had not been home for about three weeks and did not have any money to send home. Finally, I got a load going home. When I got home, I only made a little money for the whole time I was out on the road. I was a little upset when I looked at my check, and I had to deal with my wife the whole time. Well, I knew that I was going to have a problem with her when I got to the apartment. I got home about noon that day and faced her. After she found out how much I brought home, she had a lot to say about it. After yelling at each other for what seemed like an eternity, I decided to quit that job that day; no need to wait and give a two-week notice. I was thinking about that "one thousand dollars" a week job now, as quiet as it had stayed! It was time to call that other fleet owner now. I made the call that Thursday morning, and I was told the position was still open and that he could send me a bus ticket. He would also meet me in Memphis, Tennessee, and then he added that I would have to make about three runs a week for that grand that he was promising. I thought to myself that should not be hard; he must be getting runs kind of regularly, that is like three runs a week. I can do that no problem! I got to downtown Atlanta that same day, the teller had my ticket, and after a little wait, my bus showed up. I got on and looked for a seat so that I could be alone. I like being by myself sometimes, and I can rest and recharge. That is what introverts do; that is what I am, an introvert. The spot I found was at the back of the bus. I had a seat to myself, lovely. As a driver, one of the things I did was watch the road and check every slow-down and turn that a driver made. It was probably a habit, but I would occasionally try to look out the front window, which was difficult from where I was seated. But to my relief, we made it safely. The truck owner told me to meet him at the pilot truck stop. I recognized him from the orientation in Ohio where we met. I then went over and greeted him, and I noticed that he had another driver with him. I was not expecting that, but I did not say anything until it was time to go because that is when I noticed that all three of us were getting into the one truck. Well, I was not comfortable with that. Three people in one truck! So, I promptly mentioned it to him and waited for an answer to this dilemma; he then explained that once we got him home, he would turn it over to the other driver and me. I was not too happy with that idea. *I am here now, and I may as well ride this horse on to see the outcome, at least until I can make some money and get the flock out of dodge.* We picked up a load at Coca-Cola in Atlanta and headed to Johnstown, New York. He had me start out, and I thought to myself, this is my test drive so that he can see if I could drive. When I began driving up the road and shifting gears, I heard him say to the other driver, who was also looking at me, "You see, that is the way you suppose to shift, not jerking the truck around with every gear." I tried to keep a straight face, but I knew that they could see the big smile growing on my face. I felt my pride building up in me, but I did know that when pride builds up, you are about to do something to mess it up, so I tried to humble myself before that could happen, but it was too late. I went to downshift and forgot what gear I was in, and as soon as I messed up, I saw the other driver look at me as though he was thinking, "See, you are not a super trucker," with a gloating look in his eyes as he smirked in triumph! Things calmed down after that as we went on our way up 75 northbound. After we got to Knoxville, Tennessee, we made a stop at Flying J Truck Stop, fueled up, took showers, and got something to eat. Then, we switched drivers. The other driver took the wheel, and I crawled up into the sleeper-birth. I took out my sleeping bag and put it on top of someone's bedding because that is what I was using while I was on the road. I took the top bunk; that is where the owner was normally to sleep, but since it was now three of us in the truck, someone had to sit up, and since I was a driver and the other driver had to have somewhere to sleep, the owner had to sit up and sleep on the passenger seat. While back there in that bunk, I was thinking, *what kind of mess is this that I have gotten myself into? When I get paid, I am going to be on my way. I cannot live like this. I got no space to myself.* Three grown men in such a small area. The next thing I remember, I was waking up because I had to go to the bathroom, so I sat up on the side of the bunk and let them know the deal. I was told no problem; they had to stop too. We stopped at a truck stop and took a little break to use the bathroom and stretch our legs, and then we were on the road again. It was starting to get dark now. Then I heard the other driver say that he could not drive at night. Now that struck me strange. This was an over-the-road tractor-trailer driver, and he said that he could not drive at night. *I have not been asleep that long, and he wanted me to get back under the wheel already? This is not going to work! As soon as I can, I am out of here.* Just then, the owner said that he was going to drive, so now I am thinking, *I guess when we take over the truck, I am going to have to do all the night driving!* I reasoned with myself that I could handle it; I did not mind driving at night. It gave me time to be to myself and recharge. The next time I woke up, we were in Tom's Brook, Virginia. We took on some fuel and got something to eat; then, I took the wheel. I drove until we were somewhere in New York. After that, the owner of the truck told me about a shortcut that he found on his GPS. The problem with that was his GPS was for cars, not for trucks, and I didn't feel right about that route. We debated about it for a while, then I told him that if he wanted to go that way, it was up to him, but I wouldn't be driving it up there. Besides, it was my break time, and I stopped and let them take the wheel, and I went to bed. Not too long after I went to sleep, I was awakened by someone touching me. I was on the top bunk in the truck, so I knew that it was an intentional touch, and it was followed by someone calling my name. It was the owner of the truck, David. Wiping my eyes so that I could see him clearly, I could not help noticing that the truck was not moving, and at that time, I heard him say that they had a problem. After getting down from the bunk, I saw that we were stopped at the mouth of a railroad bridge they intended to go under. I got in the driver's seat and rolled down the window. I stuck my body partway out of it so that I could see the top of the truck and the bottom of the bridge; something that I remembered from tractor-trailer school called a Bridge Clearance Check. I put one foot on the brake and let the truck slowly roll forward to see how much room there was in between them. I saw that it was not enough, so the next thing to do was to back the truck up and find another way around the bridge. While backing up, I saw another road to my left, but it had a sign on it that said no trucks. I told them that I would have to back some more because 'no trucks' were supposed to be on that one. And to my surprise, David, the owner of the truck, told me that the road that said 'no trucks' was the way that they came in! I am thinking to myself, *now I better get away from these guys; neither one of them knows what they are doing!* But we finally got to the delivery point and got unloaded. After we got done, we did not have a load, so we went to a nearby truck stop; this one was close to where I once lived before moving to Georgia. I kept thinking that maybe I should just head on over there and let this job go, but I was still not paid, so I had no money, and my wife was still in Atlanta. We had to layover at that truck stop until we found another load, so we took that opportunity to get a fresh shower and something to eat. We even had time to watch a movie. This truck stop had a nice little movie theater in it. After a little bit, we were dispatched out on a load going to California. So, we picked up the load and started out for Fontana, California. On the way, the other driver got his electric razor out and proceeded to shave. I thought it was strange that he would do this every day without fail. Yet, I received no pay, and the owner of the truck kept saying that I would have to make three runs before I could get paid. Fast forward, we made it to Fontana, California. The place was littered with trucks; it was an unpaved parking lot next to a house. A guy and a young lady came out to meet us, and I remember seeing the lady at the orientation in Ohio. We gave them the trailer, and the owner of the truck and the couple that came out to meet us got together and started talking. After they finished with their meeting, we headed out. The truck owner said we were going to his house in Vegas for a break, and I assumed that once we arrived and rested, he would let the other driver and I go to work. It was a nice size house with a pool in the backyard; the pool boy was cleaning as we arrived, and we looked through the double glass doors in the rear of the kitchen where his wife was preparing some food. He showed us our rooms and let us know that we would be eating soon, so if we wanted to take a shower, there was plenty of time. After we ate, we went to the garage where he had two cars parked: a BMW and a Lexis, both in good condition. He had them both parked outside of the two-car garage in the driveway. We got in the BMW and headed off to downtown Las Vegas. He gave us the grand tour; I saw a motorcycle with handlebars fashioned like the Medusa, and outside there was a big boat that looked like a pirate ship, and it was right in front of a building. We went across the street and into a building that had a water fountain in front of it with multiple fountains squirting water in the air with colorful lights that changed every so often, giving the fountains a special glow in the dark. There were people milling around all over the place. We went to Gilley's Bar, had a couple of beers, and looked around in the casinos. They had them everywhere, but I did not gamble. After going here and there, we were ready to get some rest. We stayed two days at his house. Then he told me that the other driver wanted to stop at his place for a break, and I thought to myself, we are spending a lot of time doing nothing. I do have a wife at home, and I need to be sending her money to take care of the bills and herself. The other driver lived in Long Beach, California. We dropped him off, and I went back to the truck. Mind you, I was in a tractor with no trailer, and I was sitting parked on the street with nowhere to go. I sat there for two days, so I was wondering why we did not have a load yet. I later found out that the owner of the truck was turning down a lot of loads. He said that they did not pay enough, but there I sat. I was so ready to get away from that setup. I was not making any money; he was still talking about how I must get three trips before I get my paycheck. My mind was made up at that point. *As soon as I get enough money, I am out of here. They can have it.* Then on the evening of the third day, we got a load. I did not care where it was going; I just wanted to get paid so I could scat! He said when I get loaded, I was to call dispatch, and they would give me an advance on the load for bills like fuel and such. After I got the load, I made the call to let dispatch know that I was ready to go. Then, I was asked about the other driver, if he was there with me. I told them that he was on his break! With urgency in his voice, he said, "No, this is a team run. There must be two of you on this one!" I told them that I would call to see when he would be ready to go. He replied that if the other driver was not going to be in the truck as well, then they would have to give the load to another team. So, I called the truck owner and explained the situation; he hurried and told me that he was going to get back to me. When he called back, he had dispatch and the other driver on the phone; dispatch called my name and asked, "Are you there?" And I replied, "Yes, I am here." Then he said to the other driver, "Are you there?" The other driver said, "Yes, I am here." Dispatch was satisfied! He thought that when the other driver said that he was there that he meant in the truck .I just wanted to get out of there so that I could get paid and go home. So, when I got on the road, the load was supposed to arrive in Utah the next morning, and I was wondering if I would make it. *Well, I would give it my best shot!* On my way up I-15 North, there was a backup! I thought to myself, *I am not going to make my appointment with this going on.* So, I got off the highway and took a side road. As I was driving, I saw something on, not in, but on the highway. As I got closer, I noticed that it was writing on the road! I was on Route 66. A famous route. I had found that route; I had heard so much about it! The highway sign was drawn on the road itself, right in the middle of the lanes. Finally, I was able to get back on I-15, a much bigger highway. I rode for a while, but now I was feeling my sleep coming down on me! I was trying with all I had to stay awake, but I knew that it was not going to be long before I would have to find a place to get a Knapp! Just then, my phone rang. It was dispatch again! I answered, and they asked me to put the other driver on. I then lied and said that he was asleep because he had to drive next! Just then, the call dropped due to a coverage problem, so I took that opportunity to call the owner of the truck to let him know what was going on. He quickly said not to answer the phone. I knew that if I answered, they were going to have someone else take the run, and I did not need that! But after a while, I had to pick up my phone and answer! I was told to take the trailer to another team; they were to take the run, and I was to get their trailer and drop it in Fontana, California. So, I did as I was told and switched trailers with the team drivers. They were a Filipino couple, and the female was doing the driving and the talking too! After the switch, I headed back down I-15 to Fontana. On my way, I asked the truck owner if I could keep the advance money to send home to my wife because I had not sent anything home for about three weeks, and she was getting anxious. He said I could, but I had to complete three runs before I got my full pay. So, I sent my wife the money before I got to Fontana. When I got to the drop-off point, they were already expecting me. They told me where to drop the trailer, and I was on my way up to Los Angeles. The owner of the truck told me that he would meet me and show me where to park the truck. We met up in Ontario, California, just outside of Los Angeles at a truck stop where I-15 and I-10 met, a TA truck stop. From there, he led me to Hawthorn, California, and we parked the truck behind a small mall that looked like it was gone out of business. The truck had no tags on it because we were not hooked up to a trailer. Little did I know that it was going to be my home for about a week or so. David would come by every now and then and give me twenty dollars or so to eat, and when I needed to use the restroom, I would go to the nearest restaurant that was open at the time. I remember one day we went to a coffee shop, and there was a guy outside that looked familiar. It was one of the drivers he had with him at the orientation in Ohio. The guy was living outside of the coffee shop; he was homeless! And the truck boss decided to take him on again so he would at least have a place to sleep. I was thinking to myself, how did he wind up in that position anyway? Just two or three weeks ago, he was driving for this company! Was this going to happen to me? Two weeks and I have not been paid yet. When I went into the restaurant to get something to eat and use the restroom, on my way back to the truck, I ran into a guy who was walking in the same direction I was. As is my habit, I struck up a conversation with him, and as we talked, he mentioned that he worked for the airport. He said that as an employee of the airport, he would receive what is called buddy passes. I asked him what it was, and he explained that he could get tickets for friends at a large discount! So, with that in mind, I asked him what kind of discount he could get me to travel from Hawthorn, California, to Rochester, New York. After thinking about it, he replied, "$98!" I did not have the money because I had sent all the money I had received to my wife. So, I told him I would have to get back to him once I had some money, and he gave me his phone number before leaving. That night, I put in a call to my wife and asked her to send me the money that I sent her last week because I had to get away from there. She told me that she didn't have it; she used it as a down payment for an apartment. I told her that I needed it to catch a flight out of there, and she said that if she could get it back, we would not be able to get the apartment and where we would live when I got there. I told her, "Look, I am living in a truck, with no tags, in the back of an abandoned mall now. I need to get out of here, I will find something when I get there, but I must leave here." After some more back and forth, she decided to send it. When I got the money, I called the guy who worked for the airport, and he told me that he would set it up and call me back. When he called back, he said that everything was set. He told me when I get to the airport to give them a code that he gave me and pay the $98, and I would be on my way. When I got back to the truck, the other driver was on the bottom bunk awake. I thought I would play it cool until he went to sleep and then sneak out, catch a bus to the airport, and be gone before morning. I did not want the truck boss to know until I was gone. He thought that he was going to keep on holding me there with the promise of a thousand dollars, but that time had passed! That is trafficking, using me as a slave! I was getting increasingly upset as I thought about it! So, I got up and started packing my stuff. The other driver was not asleep yet, but I did not care anymore! I was going, and nobody was going to stop me; I was afraid that if anyone tried to stop me, someone would get hurt! After packing my stuff, I headed to the bus stop. I did not even know if that was the right bus, but I was going. I was thinking to myself, *if anyone tries to stop me, some dreadful things will happen. I am not staying any longer; it is a done deal!* After a little bit, a bus showed up, and as I got on, I asked the bus driver, "Where do I catch a bus that goes to the airport?" He looked at me, smiled, and said, "You are on it!" That was a relief. I was now on my way back home. On the ride to the airport, I was starting to feel like a terrible experience was now over.

Then, I started thinking, *this is my first time on an airplane! I hope I do not panic or otherwise act a fool! I have seen on television and in movies how people on their first flight trip out! But whatever, I am going on with it.* After getting on the other side of the check-in line, I thought to myself that it was not bad at all; *now to find my flight!* When I reached my gate, they were already looking for me. They said that they were about to close the door. I found my seat, there was a couple seated in two of the spots, and I was supposed to be in the middle of them, but they asked me if I would not mind switching seats with one of them, and they gave me a window seat! I thought, *Yeah, Boy!* My first time on an airplane! It was not that bad, but we had not taken off yet. The plane started to move, and I felt the excitement buildup in my heart. I started looking out the window, and I was right over the left wing. We started rolling, and then I felt the weight of my body being pulled down into the seat. This was it, and we were leaving the ground. I was seated near the window over the left wing, and as we went over the water, I realized that we were flying over the Pacific Ocean. And then we began to turn left, and the wing where my seat was beginning to point down at the ocean, and as I looked across the water, I saw California shrinking until I was looking down at just the water. We then headed back towards the land, but we were going higher in the air, and we kept going higher until we were in the clouds. I was on my way back to Rochester. It was quiet for a while. The only sound was the hum of the jets and the chatter of the people on the jet. Out the window, I was looking at another jet going in the other direction, and you could see what looked like a shadow trail behind it. It looked like we were moving slowly, but I knew we were not. After a while, it was out of site, and there were only clouds to look at, and I did for a bit. Then I felt the jet begin to slow down and a light feeling in my stomach, meaning that the jet was going down. I then heard a noise and knew it was the sound of the landing gear, meaning that we were about to land. I thought, this can't be Rochester already. Looking out of the window, I could see the ground. It looked like a patchwork, like on a quilt. As we got closer, I could see roads, buildings, houses, and cars, but I did not recognize where we were. I found out that it was Philadelphia, a stop-off to change planes. When we were on the ground, we started to unload. Inside the airport, people were milling around like a colony of ants. I had to find where my connecting flight was loading. After I got on my plane, I noticed that it was much smaller than the first one, and the engines were louder too! But we finally got ready to take off. I finally made it to Rochester early in the morning on February 2nd, 2010. When my bags got to me, I could not find my sleeping bag; it must have fallen off my duffel bag where I had it, and the people said that if it did not have a tag on it, I could forget it! So, I forgot about it like they said and headed out of the airport. Outside the airport, I noticed that it was very cold, unlike California's weather. I went over to a payphone to call my mom for a place to stay until my first paycheck. My old job had called me back and said I could start work on the 8th, and I could not stay with my wife because she was staying with her son and his wife. I did not think I would be able to stay there either, based on how my mother sounded on the phone, so I called for emergency assistance to find somewhere to stay until I could get back on my feet. They put me up in a homeless shelter, and there were all kinds of people there, from parolees to vagrants and such there too. I was told that the first thing the next day, I was to go down to social services to get food stamps and an application for an apartment, and I did that on the third and got the stamps, but I had to find the apartment. I remember taking a shower. It was like being in prison; it was a group shower situation, with no privacy whatsoever! Food was like whatever was donated, but I had to eat it until my stamps were loaded on my card. I had to sleep with all my belongings under my bed to protect them, and when I would leave the building for anything, I had to take them with me. I was told every morning that I had to get up and go look for a job. I told them I had a job starting on the 8th, but they still wanted everyone out looking every day. I was overjoyed when the 8th arrived because it meant I could finally start working. So, I had Johnny, who was a co-worker and the best man at my wedding about a year before, come and pick me up and drop me off for work. I was so ashamed for him to pick me up at a homeless shelter every day, but I had to do what I had to do until I could do better. The good thing about going back to this job was that I did not have to be trained again. I knew just what and how to do the job at hand. My wife told me about an apartment she found that sounded like it would be a delightful place for me, so we made an appointment to meet with the Landlord. On the 12th of February 2018, I moved into that apartment, and my wife moved back in with me. So, I was back in Rochester, back at the job I had before I left about a year and a half ago, and my wife was back with me. Any more of this story would have to be in another book.